ADULT MONEY

Personal Finance Guide to Adulting

David Klipsch

Copyright © 2024 David Klipsch

All rights reserved

The characters and events portrayed in this book are fictitious. Any similarity to real persons, living or dead, is coincidental and not intended by the author.

No part of this book may be reproduced, or stored in a retrieval system, or transmitted in any form or by any means, electronic, mechanical, photocopying, recording, or otherwise, without express written permission of the publisher.

Disclaimer:
This book is for informational purposes only, you should not take any part of the book as legal, tax, or financial advice.

Investing comes with risk and do not invest in any asset without doing your own research.

CONTENTS

Title Page
Copyright
Chapter 1: Understanding Your Financial Situation   1
Chapter 2: Budgeting and Saving   5
Chapter 3: Managing Debt   16
Chapter 4: Investing Basics   23
Chapter 5: Building Wealth Through Investments   28
Chapter 6: Protecting Your Finances   38
Chapter 7: Building Multiple Streams of Income   47
Chapter 8: Planning for Major Financial Milestones   59
Chapter 9: Retirement Planning   65
Chapter 10 Real World Scenarios   72
Chapter 11: Achieving Financial Freedom   84
About The Author   91

CHAPTER 1: UNDERSTANDING YOUR FINANCIAL SITUATION

Before you embark on the journey to financial success, it's crucial to have a clear understanding of your current financial situation. This chapter will guide you through assessing your finances, tracking your income and expenses, calculating your net worth, and setting achievable financial goals.

Assessing Your Current Financial Status:

Assessing your current financial status involves taking stock of various aspects of your financial health. Start by evaluating your income sources. This includes your primary income from wages or salary, as well as any additional sources such as bonuses, investments, rental income, or side hustles. Knowing how much money is coming in each month forms the foundation of your financial plan.

Next, examine your expenses. It's important to distinguish between fixed expenses, such as rent or mortgage payments, utilities, insurance premiums, and loan repayments, and variable expenses, such as groceries, dining out, entertainment, and discretionary spending. Understanding where your money is going will help you identify areas where you can potentially cut back and save.

Debt is another crucial aspect of your financial picture. Make a list of all your outstanding debts, including credit card balances, student loans, car loans, personal loans, and mortgages. Note the interest rates, minimum payments, and outstanding balances for each debt. Understanding your debt burden will allow you to develop strategies for repayment and avoid accruing unnecessary interest charges.

Finally, take stock of your assets. These may include cash savings, retirement accounts, investment portfolios, real estate properties, vehicles, valuable possessions, and any other assets of value. Calculate the total value of your assets and compare it to your total liabilities (debts) to determine your net worth. A positive net worth indicates that your assets exceed your debts, while a negative net worth signals that you owe more than you own.

Tracking Your Income and Expenses:

Once you've assessed your financial situation, it's essential to track your income and expenses regularly. This process involves recording all sources of income and categorizing your expenditures to understand where your money is going. You can use various tools and methods to track your finances, including spreadsheets, budgeting apps, or dedicated financial software.

Start by listing all sources of income, including wages, salary, bonuses, dividends, interest, rental income, and any other sources of revenue. Then, categorize your expenses into essential categories (such as housing, utilities, groceries, transportation, insurance, and debt repayments) and discretionary categories (such as dining out, entertainment, travel, and shopping). Be thorough in your tracking to capture all expenses accurately.

Tracking your income and expenses will provide valuable insights into your spending habits and patterns. You may discover areas where you're overspending or identify opportunities to cut back and save. Regularly reviewing your financial transactions will help you stay accountable to your budget and adjust as needed to align your spending with your financial goals.

Calculating Your Net Worth:

Your net worth is a measure of your financial health and represents the difference between your assets and liabilities. Calculating your net worth provides a snapshot of your overall financial situation and helps you track your progress over time. To calculate your net worth, subtract your total liabilities (debts) from your total assets.

Assets may include cash savings, investment accounts, retirement funds, real estate properties, vehicles, valuable possessions, and any other assets with monetary value. Liabilities consist of outstanding debts, such as credit card balances, student loans, car loans, personal loans, and mortgages. Subtracting your total liabilities from your total assets will give you your net worth.

Regularly monitoring your net worth allows you to track your financial progress and make adjustments to your financial plan as needed. Aim to increase your net worth over time by paying down debt, increasing savings and investments, and growing your assets. By focusing on improving your net worth, you'll build a solid foundation for long-term financial success.

Setting Financial Goals:

Setting clear and achievable financial goals is essential for guiding your financial decisions and keeping you motivated on your financial journey. Your goals should be specific, measurable, achievable, relevant, and time-bound (SMART). Whether your goals are short-term, medium-term, or long-term, they should reflect your priorities and values.

Start by identifying your financial objectives and aspirations. These may include saving for emergencies, paying off debt, buying a home, funding education, investing for retirement, or achieving financial independence. Once you've identified your goals, break them down into smaller, actionable steps with deadlines attached. This will make them more manageable and increase your likelihood of success.

Write down your financial goals and review them regularly to stay focused and motivated. Consider creating a vision board or visual representation of your goals to keep them at the forefront of your mind. Share your goals with a trusted friend, family member, or financial advisor for accountability and support. As you achieve each goal, celebrate your progress, and set new goals to continue moving forward on your financial journey.

Conclusion:

Understanding your financial situation is the first step toward taking control of your finances and building a secure future. By assessing your current financial status, tracking your income and expenses, calculating your net worth, and setting SMART financial goals, you'll be well-equipped to make informed decisions and work towards achieving financial stability and prosperity. In the subsequent chapters, we'll delve deeper into strategies for budgeting, saving, investing, and planning for major financial milestones. Remember, your financial journey is unique, and progress may take time, but with dedication and perseverance, you can achieve your financial goals and create the life of abundance you desire.

CHAPTER 2: BUDGETING AND SAVING

Budgeting and saving are essential components of financial health and security. They provide the foundation for achieving financial goals, whether it's buying a house, funding education, or preparing for retirement. In this chapter, we'll delve deep into the importance of budgeting, explore effective budgeting strategies, and discuss practical tips for saving money.

The Importance of Budgeting:

Budgeting is the process of creating a plan for how you will allocate your income to cover your expenses and achieve your financial goals. Here's why budgeting is crucial:

1. Financial Awareness:

Budgeting helps you understand your financial situation by providing a clear overview of your income and expenses. It allows you to see where your money is going, identify spending patterns, and make informed decisions about your finances.

2. Goal Setting:

A budget serves as a roadmap for achieving your financial goals. Whether you want to pay off debt, save for a vacation, or build an emergency fund, a budget helps you allocate resources towards your goals and track your progress over time.

3. Expense Control:

By tracking your spending and adhering to a budget, you can control your expenses and avoid overspending. Budgeting encourages mindful spending habits and helps you differentiate between needs and wants.

4. Debt Management:
Budgeting is an effective tool for managing debt. By allocating funds towards debt repayment each month, you can accelerate your progress towards becoming debt-free and save money on interest charges.

5. Financial Security:
Budgeting helps you build a financial safety net and prepare for unexpected expenses or emergencies. By setting aside funds for savings and creating an emergency fund, you can protect yourself from financial setbacks and weather financial storms.

Creating a Budget That Works for You:

Creating a budget that aligns with your financial goals and lifestyle requires careful planning and attention to detail. Here's a step-by-step guide to creating an effective budget:

1. Calculate Your Income:
Start by determining your total monthly income from all sources, including wages, salary, bonuses, freelance work, investment income, and any other sources of revenue. Make sure to include all sources of income to get an accurate picture of your financial resources.

2. List Your Expenses:
Next, make a list of all your monthly expenses, categorizing them into fixed and variable expenses. Fixed expenses are recurring costs that remain relatively constant each month, such as rent or mortgage payments, utilities, insurance premiums, and loan payments. Variable expenses, on the other hand, fluctuate from month to month and include groceries, dining out, entertainment, transportation, and discretionary spending.

3. Differentiate Between Needs and Wants:
Review your list of expenses and distinguish between essential needs and discretionary wants. Needs are items or services that

are necessary for your basic survival and well-being, such as food, shelter, clothing, transportation, and healthcare. Wants, on the other hand, are non-essential items or services that you desire but can live without, such as luxury goods, entertainment, travel, and dining out.

4. Set Budget Categories:
Allocate a specific amount of money to each budget category based on your income and expenses. Start by covering your needs first, such as housing, utilities, groceries, and transportation, before allocating funds to discretionary categories. Be realistic in your allocations and leave room for unexpected expenses or fluctuations.

5. Track Your Spending:
Once you've created your budget, track your spending throughout the month to ensure you stay within your budgeted amounts. Keep receipts, use budgeting apps or software, or create a spreadsheet to monitor your expenses and compare them to your budgeted amounts. Tracking your spending in real-time allows you to identify areas where you may be overspending and make adjustments as needed to stay on track.

6. Review and Adjust:
At the end of each month, review your budget and assess your spending habits. Compare your actual expenses to your budgeted amounts and identify any discrepancies. Look for areas where you exceeded your budget and consider adjustments you can make to stay within your budgeted amounts in the future. Make adjustments to your budget as necessary to reflect changes in your financial situation or priorities.

50/30/20 Budget
The 50/30/20 budgeting rule is a simple and popular framework for managing personal finances. It suggests allocating your after-tax income into three broad categories: needs, wants, and savings. Here's how it works:

50% for Needs:

- Allocate 50% of your after-tax income towards covering your essential needs. These include expenses that are necessary for your basic survival and well-being, such as:
    - Housing (rent/mortgage, utilities, property taxes, insurance)
    - Food (groceries, essential household items)
    - Transportation (car payments, public transportation, gas, insurance)
    - Healthcare (health insurance premiums, medical expenses, prescriptions)
    - Minimum debt payments (minimum payments on credit cards, student loans, personal loans, etc.)
- The idea is to ensure that you prioritize covering your essential expenses first, as they are critical for maintaining a basic standard of living.

30% for Wants:

- Allocate 30% of your after-tax income towards discretionary spending on wants or non-essential expenses. These are expenses that enhance your lifestyle or provide enjoyment but are not strictly necessary for survival. Examples of wants include:
    - Dining out at restaurants
    - Entertainment (movies, concerts, streaming services)
    - Travel/vacations
    - Hobbies and leisure activities
    - Non-essential clothing and accessories
- This category allows you to enjoy some of the finer things in life while still being mindful of your overall financial health.

20% for Savings and Debt Repayment:

- Allocate 20% of your after-tax income towards savings, investments, and debt repayment. This category is critical for building wealth, achieving financial goals, and securing your financial future. It includes:
    - Emergency fund savings
    - Retirement Savings (401(k), IRA, etc.)
    - Investment accounts (stocks, bonds, mutual funds, ETFs)
    - Debt repayment (accelerating payments beyond the minimum, paying off high-interest debt)
- Prioritizing savings and debt repayment in this category ensures that you're building a financial safety net, preparing for the future, and making progress towards financial independence.

The 50/30/20 budgeting rule provides a simple and flexible framework for managing your finances. It encourages you to prioritize your spending based on your needs, wants, and savings goals, while also allowing for some degree of flexibility and discretion within each category. However, it's essential to adjust the percentages based on your individual financial situation, goals, and lifestyle preferences. Additionally, regular monitoring and adjustments to your budget are necessary to ensure that it remains aligned with your financial priorities and objectives.

Zero based Budgeting

Zero-based budgeting (ZBB) is a budgeting approach where all expenses must be justified for each new period, regardless of whether the expense has occurred in the previous period. In other words, it requires that every dollar of income is allocated to a specific expense or savings category, leaving no money unaccounted for. The primary goal of zero-based budgeting is to optimize the allocation of resources and ensure that funds are used efficiently to support strategic objectives.

Here's how zero-based budgeting works:

1. Start from Zero:
Unlike traditional budgeting methods where the previous period's budget serves as the starting point, zero-based budgeting starts from scratch. Each department or individual must justify all expenses, regardless of whether they were included in the previous budget or not.

2. Identify Needs and Priorities:
The budgeting process begins by identifying the organization's or individual's needs, priorities, and objectives for the upcoming period. This involves assessing current operations, evaluating strategic goals, and determining the resources required to achieve desired outcomes.

3. Categorize Expenses:
Expenses are categorized based on their nature and purpose, such as personnel costs, overhead expenses, marketing expenses, research and development costs, etc. Each expense category is then evaluated to determine its necessity and alignment with organizational goals.

4. Assign Budgets:
Once expenses are categorized, budget allocations are determined for each category based on the identified needs and priorities. Budgets are typically set at the level required to achieve desired outcomes efficiently, rather than simply adjusting the previous period's budget up or down.

5. Justify Expenses:
Each department or individual is required to justify all expenses within their budget, providing detailed explanations of why each expense is necessary to support organizational objectives. This ensures transparency and accountability in the budgeting process.

6. Continuous Monitoring and Review:

Throughout the budget period, expenses are closely monitored to ensure that actual spending aligns with the allocated budget. Any significant variances are investigated, and adjustments may be made to reallocate resources as needed to address changing priorities or unforeseen circumstances.

Zero-based budgeting offers several benefits, including:

- **Resource Optimization:** By requiring a thorough justification of all expenses, zero-based budgeting helps identify inefficiencies and unnecessary costs, leading to better resource allocation and utilization.
- **Alignment with Strategic Objectives:** The budgeting process is closely tied to organizational goals and objectives, ensuring that resources are allocated in support of strategic priorities.
- **Increased Accountability:** Departments and individuals are held accountable for their spending decisions, as they must justify all expenses based on their contribution to organizational objectives.
- **Flexibility and Adaptability:** Zero-based budgeting allows for greater flexibility to adjust budgets in response to changing circumstances or priorities, enabling organizations to adapt more effectively to evolving market conditions or internal challenges.

However, zero-based budgeting also has some potential drawbacks, including:

- **Time and Resource Intensive:** The detailed nature of zero-based budgeting requires significant time and effort to implement, as each expense must be justified individually. This can be resource-intensive and may not be practical for all organizations or individuals.
- **Short-term Focus:** Zero-based budgeting tends to focus on short-term planning and may overlook longer-term strategic considerations or investments.

- **Resistance to Change:** Implementing zero-based budgeting may encounter resistance from departments or individuals accustomed to traditional budgeting methods, as it requires a shift in mindset and approach to budgeting.

Overall, zero-based budgeting can be a valuable tool for organizations and individuals looking to optimize resource allocation, improve accountability, and align spending with strategic priorities. However, it requires careful planning, commitment, and ongoing monitoring to realize its full benefits effectively.

Tips for Saving Money:

Saving money is a critical aspect of financial success, allowing you to build wealth, achieve financial goals, and prepare for the future. Here are some practical tips for saving money:

1. Pay Yourself First:
Treat savings as a non-negotiable expense and prioritize it in your budget. Set up automatic transfers from your checking account to your savings account each month to ensure consistent contributions. Paying yourself first ensures that savings are a priority and not an afterthought.

2. Reduce Discretionary Spending:
Identify areas where you can cut back on non-essential expenses, such as dining out, entertainment, shopping, and subscription services. Look for opportunities to enjoy frugal alternatives or eliminate unnecessary expenses altogether. Cutting back on discretionary spending frees up more money for savings and helps you live within your means.

3. Comparison Shop:
Before making a purchase, compare prices from multiple retailers or providers to ensure you're getting the best deal. Take advantage of discounts, coupons, and sales to save money on everyday

purchases. Whether you're shopping for groceries, clothing, electronics, or household goods, comparison shopping can help you stretch your dollars further.

4. Limit Impulse Buys:
Avoid impulse purchases by implementing a waiting period before making non-essential purchases. Give yourself time to consider whether the item is truly necessary and fits within your budget. Delaying gratification allows you to make more thoughtful purchasing decisions and avoid buyer's remorse.

5. Negotiate Bills and Expenses:
Don't be afraid to negotiate with service providers or creditors to lower your bills or interest rates. Whether it's negotiating lower rates on utilities, insurance premiums, or credit card interest charges, every dollar saved adds up over time. Be proactive about seeking out opportunities to reduce your expenses and save money.

6. Save Windfalls and Bonuses:
Whenever you receive unexpected income, such as a tax refund, bonus, or gift, consider saving a portion of it instead of spending it immediately. Use windfalls to boost your savings, pay down debt, or accelerate progress towards your financial goals. While it's tempting to splurge when you come into extra money, saving it can have a more significant impact on your financial future.

Building an Emergency Fund:

An emergency fund is a financial safety net that provides a buffer against unexpected expenses or income disruptions. It's designed to cover essential expenses, such as housing, food, utilities, and transportation, in the event of a financial emergency. Here's how to build and maintain an emergency fund:

1. Set a Savings Goal:
Start by setting a savings goal for your emergency fund. Aim to save at least three to six months' worth of living expenses to cover your basic needs in case of an emergency. Adjust your savings goal

based on your individual circumstances, such as income stability, family size, and monthly expenses.

2. Start Small:
If you're unable to save a significant amount initially, start small and gradually increase your contributions over time. Even small, regular contributions can add up over time and provide peace of mind knowing you have a financial safety net in place. Set up automatic transfers from your checking account to your emergency fund to ensure consistent contributions.

3. Keep Funds Accessible:
Keep your emergency fund in a liquid, easily accessible account, such as a high-yield savings account or money market account. Avoid investing your emergency fund in assets that may be difficult to liquidate quickly in case of an emergency. While it's essential to earn a competitive interest rate on your savings, liquidity and accessibility are paramount when it comes to your emergency fund.

4. Only Use for Emergencies:
Reserve your emergency fund for true emergencies, such as medical expenses, car repairs, job loss, or unexpected home repairs. Avoid dipping into your emergency fund for non-essential expenses or discretionary purchases. Having a designated emergency fund ensures that you have the financial resources to weather unexpected financial storms without derailing your long-term financial goals.

5. Replenish as Needed:
If you need to use funds from your emergency fund, make it a priority to replenish them as soon as possible. Adjust your budget and savings goals to accommodate replenishing your emergency fund until it reaches its target balance again. Treating replenishing your emergency fund as a non-negotiable expense ensures that you always maintain a strong financial safety net.

Conclusion:

Budgeting and saving are essential habits for achieving financial success and security. By creating a budget that aligns with your financial goals and lifestyle, practicing mindful spending habits, and prioritizing savings, you can take control of your finances and work towards a brighter financial future. Building an emergency fund provides a crucial safety net to protect you from unexpected expenses or income disruptions and ensures that you have the financial resources to weather financial storms without derailing your long-term financial goals. Start implementing these strategies today to take control of your financial future and enjoy peace of mind knowing you're on the path to financial success.

CHAPTER 3: MANAGING DEBT

Debt can be a significant financial burden, impacting your ability to achieve financial goals and build wealth. In this chapter, we'll explore strategies for effectively managing debt, including understanding different types of debt, developing a debt repayment plan, strategies for paying off debt faster, and avoiding common debt traps.

Understanding Different Types of Debt:

Not all debt is created equal, and it's essential to understand the different types of debt and their implications for your financial health. Here are some common types of debt:

1. Consumer Debt:
Consumer debt includes debts incurred for personal or household expenses, such as credit card debt, personal loans, and payday loans. Consumer debt often carries high-interest rates, making it one of the most expensive forms of debt.

2. Student Loans:
Student loans are used to finance higher education expenses, including tuition, fees, and living expenses. While student loans typically offer more favorable terms than other forms of debt, such as lower interest rates and flexible repayment options, they can still represent a significant financial obligation for borrowers.

3. Mortgages:
A mortgage is a loan used to finance the purchase of a home. Mortgages are typically long-term loans with fixed or adjustable

interest rates. While mortgages allow individuals to purchase homes without paying the full purchase price upfront, they also come with the risk of foreclosure if the borrower fails to make timely payments.

4. Auto Loans:
Auto loans are used to finance the purchase of a vehicle. Like mortgages, auto loans can be long-term loans with fixed or adjustable interest rates. While auto loans provide individuals with the ability to purchase vehicles, they may not be able to afford outright, they also come with the risk of repossession if the borrower fails to make payments.

Developing a Debt Repayment Plan:

Developing a debt repayment plan is essential for effectively managing debt and achieving financial freedom. Here are steps to create a debt repayment plan:

1. Assess Your Debt:
Start by making a list of all your debts, including the outstanding balance, interest rate, minimum monthly payment, and due date. Organize your debts from the highest interest rate to the lowest interest rate.

2. Prioritize High-Interest Debt:
Focus on paying off high-interest debt first, as it can be the most expensive and take the longest to repay. Consider strategies such as the debt avalanche method, where you allocate extra payments towards the debt with the highest interest rate while making minimum payments on other debts.

3. Consider Debt Consolidation:
If you have multiple high-interest debts, consider consolidating them into a single loan with a lower interest rate. Debt consolidation can simplify your finances and reduce your overall interest costs, making it easier to manage and pay off your debt.

4. Create a Budget:

Develop a budget that allocates a portion of your income towards debt repayment each month. Be realistic about your expenses and prioritize debt repayment in your budget to ensure that you're making progress towards paying off your debt.

5. Increase Your Income:
Consider ways to increase your income, such as taking on a side hustle, freelancing, or asking for a raise at work. Allocating extra income towards debt repayment can help you pay off your debt faster and save money on interest charges.

Strategies for Paying Off Debt Faster:

Paying off debt faster requires dedication, discipline, and a strategic approach. Here are some strategies for accelerating debt repayment:

1. Make Extra Payments:
Allocate any extra money, such as tax refunds, bonuses, or gifts, towards debt repayment. Making extra payments can help you pay off your debt faster and save money on interest charges.

2. Use the Debt Snowball Method:
The debt snowball method involves paying off debts in order from smallest to largest balance, regardless of interest rate. As you pay off each debt, you roll the payment into the next debt, creating momentum and motivation to continue paying off your debt.

3. Cut Expenses:
Look for ways to cut expenses and free up more money for debt repayment. Consider downsizing your living space, reducing discretionary spending, or eliminating non-essential expenses until your debt is paid off.

4. Negotiate Lower Interest Rates:
Contact your creditors and ask if they're willing to lower your interest rates. A lower interest rate can reduce your monthly payments and save you money on interest charges over time, making it easier to pay off your debt faster.

Avoiding Common Debt Traps:

Avoiding common debt traps is essential for staying on track with your debt repayment goals and achieving financial freedom. Here are some common debt traps to watch out for:

1. Using Credit Cards for Everyday Expenses:
Relying on credit cards to cover everyday expenses can lead to high-interest debt and make it challenging to pay off your balance in full each month. Instead, use cash or debit cards for everyday purchases to avoid accumulating unnecessary debt.

2. Ignoring Minimum Payments:
Ignoring minimum payments can result in late fees, penalties, and damage to your credit score. Always make at least the minimum payment on your debts each month to avoid additional charges and maintain a positive credit history.

3. Borrowing to Pay Off Debt:
Taking out new loans or using credit cards to pay off existing debt can be a dangerous cycle that leads to more debt. Instead of borrowing to pay off debt, focus on developing a sustainable repayment plan and sticking to it until your debt is paid off in full.

4. Falling for Predatory Lending Practices:
Be wary of lenders who offer loans with high-interest rates, hidden fees, or unfavorable terms. Do your research, read the fine print, and avoid lenders who engage in predatory lending practices that can trap you in a cycle of debt.

Debt Snowball vs Debt Avalanche:

Debt snowball and debt avalanche are two popular methods for paying off debt, each with its own approach and benefits. Let's explore the differences between the two:

Debt Snowball Method:

How it works:

The debt snowball method involves paying off debts in order from smallest to largest balance, regardless of interest rate. You make minimum payments on all debts except the smallest one, on which you focus all extra funds available.

Psychological Benefit:
The debt snowball method provides a psychological boost as you quickly eliminate smaller debts, creating momentum and motivation to continue paying off larger debts.

Example:
Let's say you have three debts: $500 on Credit Card A, $2,000 on Credit Card B, and $5,000 on a Personal Loan. You would focus on paying off Credit Card A first, even if it has the lowest interest rate, while making minimum payments on the other debts.

Benefits:
The debt snowball method can be effective for individuals who need the psychological boost of seeing progress quickly. It provides a sense of accomplishment as debts are paid off, which can help maintain motivation throughout the debt repayment process.

Debt Avalanche Method:

How it works:
The debt avalanche method involves paying off debts in order from highest to lowest interest rate, regardless of balance size. You allocate extra funds towards the debt with the highest interest rate while making minimum payments on other debts.

Interest Savings:
The debt avalanche method focuses on minimizing interest costs over time by targeting high-interest debts first. By paying off debts with the highest interest rates, you can save money on interest charges and pay off your debt faster.

Example:
Using the same example as before, if Credit Card A has a 15%

interest rate, Credit Card B has a 20% interest rate, and the Personal Loan has a 10% interest rate, you would focus on paying off Credit Card B first, as it has the highest interest rate.

Benefits:

The debt avalanche method can save you money on interest charges over time, making it a more cost-effective approach for individuals who are primarily concerned with minimizing interest costs.

Comparison:

- **Psychological vs. Financial:** The primary difference between the debt snowball and debt avalanche methods lies in their approach to debt repayment. The debt snowball method focuses on providing a psychological boost by paying off smaller debts first, while the debt avalanche method prioritizes minimizing interest costs by targeting high-interest debts.

- **Effectiveness:** Both methods are effective for paying off debt, but the best approach depends on your individual preferences and financial goals. If you need the motivation of quick wins to stay on track with your debt repayment plan, the debt snowball method may be more suitable. However, if you're primarily focused on minimizing interest costs and paying off debt as efficiently as possible, the debt avalanche method may be a better fit.

- **Personalization:** Some individuals may choose to combine elements of both methods and tailor their approach based on their specific financial situation. For example, you could start with the debt snowball method to gain momentum and then switch to the debt avalanche method once you've eliminated smaller debts.

In conclusion, both the debt snowball and debt avalanche

methods offer effective strategies for paying off debt. The key is to choose the approach that aligns with your financial goals, motivations, and preferences, and to stay disciplined and committed to your debt repayment plan.

Conclusion:

Managing debt effectively is essential for achieving financial freedom and building wealth. By understanding different types of debt, developing a debt repayment plan, employing strategies for paying off debt faster, and avoiding common debt traps, you can take control of your finances and work towards a debt-free future. Remember, managing debt is a journey that requires dedication, discipline, and perseverance, but the rewards of financial freedom and peace of mind are well worth the effort.

CHAPTER 4: INVESTING BASICS

Investing is a crucial aspect of building wealth and achieving financial goals. Whether you're saving for retirement, funding your children's education, or building a nest egg for the future, investing can help you grow your money over time. In this chapter, we'll explore the fundamentals of investing, including different investment vehicles, strategies for building a diversified portfolio, and essential principles for successful investing.

Understanding Investment Vehicles:

Investment vehicles are assets or instruments that individuals can invest in to grow their money. Here are some common investment vehicles:

Stocks:
Stocks represent ownership in a company and are bought and sold on stock exchanges. When you buy a stock, you become a shareholder in the company and are entitled to a portion of its profits through dividends and capital appreciation.
Stocks offer the potential for high returns but also come with higher risk and volatility compared to other investment options. It's essential to research and diversify your stock investments to minimize risk.

Bonds:
Bonds are debt securities issued by governments, municipalities, or corporations to raise capital. When you buy a bond, you're essentially lending money to the issuer in exchange for periodic interest payments and the return of the principal amount at

maturity.

Bonds are considered safer and less volatile than stocks, making them suitable for investors seeking income and capital preservation. However, they typically offer lower returns compared to stocks.

Mutual Funds:
Mutual funds are investment vehicles that pool money from multiple investors to invest in a diversified portfolio of stocks, bonds, or other assets. They're managed by professional fund managers, who make investment decisions on behalf of investors. Mutual funds offer diversification, professional management, and convenience, making them popular investment choices for individual investors. They come in various types, including equity funds, bond funds, index funds, and target-date funds.

Exchange-Traded Funds (ETFs):
ETFs are similar to mutual funds but trade on stock exchanges like individual stocks. They offer the diversification of mutual funds with the flexibility and liquidity of stocks.

ETFs track various indexes, sectors, or asset classes and can be an efficient way to gain exposure to specific market segments or investment themes. They typically have lower expense ratios compared to mutual funds.

Real Estate:
Real estate investment involves purchasing properties, such as residential homes, commercial buildings, or rental properties, with the expectation of generating rental income and/or capital appreciation.

Real estate offers the potential for passive income, tax advantages, and portfolio diversification. However, it requires significant capital investment, ongoing maintenance, and may be less liquid compared to other investment options.

Building a Diversified Portfolio:

Diversification is a fundamental principle of investing that involves spreading your investments across different asset classes, industries, and geographic regions to reduce risk and enhance returns. Here are some strategies for building a diversified portfolio:

Asset Allocation:
Asset allocation involves determining the mix of asset classes (stocks, bonds, cash, real estate, etc.) in your investment portfolio. The appropriate asset allocation depends on factors such as your investment goals, risk tolerance, time horizon, and financial situation.
A well-diversified portfolio typically includes a mix of stocks, bonds, and cash or cash equivalents. The specific allocation will vary based on individual circumstances and investment objectives.

Stock Sector Diversification:
Within the stock portion of your portfolio, diversify across different sectors of the economy to reduce sector-specific risk. For example, allocate investments across sectors such as technology, healthcare, consumer goods, financials, and utilities.
Sector diversification helps mitigate the impact of adverse events or economic downturns affecting specific industries.

International Diversification:
Diversify your investments geographically by including international stocks and bonds in your portfolio. Investing in foreign markets provides exposure to different economies, currencies, and geopolitical factors, reducing the risk of being overly concentrated in any single country or region.
International diversification can also enhance portfolio returns by tapping into growth opportunities in emerging markets.

Alternative Investments:
Consider including alternative investments, such as real estate, commodities, or hedge funds, in your portfolio to further diversify risk and enhance returns. Alternative investments have

low correlation with traditional asset classes like stocks and bonds, providing additional diversification benefits.

However, alternative investments may be less liquid, more complex, and carry higher fees compared to traditional investments, so it's essential to research and understand the risks involved.

Essential Principles for Successful Investing:

Successful investing requires discipline, patience, and adherence to fundamental principles. Here are some essential principles to keep in mind:

Start Early and Invest Regularly:

Time is one of the most powerful factors in investing due to the compounding effect of returns. Start investing as early as possible and contribute regularly to take advantage of the power of compounding.

Even small, consistent investments can grow significantly over time, thanks to the exponential growth of compound returns.

Set Clear Investment Goals:

Define your investment goals, such as retirement planning, saving for a home, or funding education expenses. Establishing clear objectives helps guide your investment decisions and ensures that your portfolio is aligned with your financial goals.

Set specific, measurable, achievable, relevant, and time-bound (SMART) goals to track your progress and stay motivated.

Diversify and Rebalance Regularly:

Diversification is key to reducing risk and achieving consistent returns. Regularly review and rebalance your portfolio to maintain the desired asset allocation and risk level.

Rebalancing involves selling investments that have appreciated in value and reinvesting the proceeds into underperforming assets to bring your portfolio back into alignment with your target asset allocation.

Stay Disciplined and Avoid Emotional Decisions:

Investing requires discipline and a long-term perspective. Avoid making impulsive decisions based on fear or greed, as emotional investing can lead to costly mistakes.

Stick to your investment plan, tune out short-term market fluctuations, and focus on your long-term goals. Maintain a diversified portfolio and stay the course, even during periods of market volatility.

Monitor Performance and Adjust as Needed:
Regularly monitor the performance of your investments and evaluate whether they're meeting your expectations. Review your investment strategy and make adjustments as needed based on changes in your financial situation, goals, or market conditions.

Stay informed about economic trends, geopolitical events, and market developments that may impact your investments. Seek advice from financial professionals or advisors if you're uncertain about investment decisions.

Conclusion:

Investing is an essential tool for building wealth, achieving financial goals, and securing your financial future. By understanding different investment vehicles, building a diversified portfolio, and adhering to essential principles for successful investing, you can maximize returns while managing risk effectively. Remember, investing is a long-term endeavor that requires patience, discipline, and a commitment to your financial goals. Start investing early, stay diversified, and stay disciplined.

CHAPTER 5: BUILDING WEALTH THROUGH INVESTMENTS

Building wealth through investments is a journey that requires patience, discipline, and a strategic approach. Whether you're saving for retirement, creating a financial legacy for your family, or pursuing financial independence, investing can help you grow your wealth over time. In this chapter, we'll explore various strategies and principles for building wealth through investments, including money prioritization with order of operations, setting investment goals, creating a diversified portfolio, harnessing the power of compounding, and navigating market volatility.

Investing Order of Operations

The order of operation for managing saving/investing accounts is specific to each persons goals and situations. In the realm of personal finance, this sequence of prioritization is crucial for optimizing your financial health and achieving long-term prosperity. I created an order that should benefit most situations. Let's delve into the fundamental order of operation for investing accounts, outlining each step's significance in securing your financial future.

1. Emergency Fund: Before venturing into the world of investing, it's imperative to establish a financial safety net in the form of an emergency fund. This pool of readily accessible cash serves as a buffer against unforeseen expenses, such as medical emergencies, car repairs, or sudden job loss. By prioritizing the creation of an emergency fund, you can safeguard yourself from the need to liquidate investments prematurely during times of crisis, thereby preserving your long-term financial goals.

2. Pay off High-Interest Debt: Once your emergency fund is in place, directing your resources towards eliminating high-interest debt should take precedence. Debts with exorbitant interest rates, such as credit card balances or payday loans, can quickly erode your financial stability and impede your progress towards wealth accumulation. By prioritizing debt repayment, you not only alleviate the burden of interest payments but also free up additional funds for future investments.

3. 401k Company Match: If your employer offers a 401(k) retirement savings plan with a matching contribution, seizing this opportunity should be a top priority. Employer matches represent free money and serve as an invaluable perk to accelerate your retirement savings. Contribute enough to your 401(k) to maximize the employer match, effectively doubling your investment returns without any additional effort.

4. Sinking Fund: Anticipated future expenses, such as home repairs, vacations, or vehicle maintenance, necessitate proactive financial planning. Establishing sinking funds for these foreseeable expenditures enables you to set aside funds gradually, ensuring you're adequately prepared when the time comes to cover these costs without resorting to debt or disrupting your investment strategy.

5. Health Savings Account (HSA): For individuals enrolled in high-deductible health insurance plans, contributing to a Health Savings Account (HSA) offers a triple tax advantage. HSA contributions are tax-deductible, grow tax-free, and withdrawals for qualified medical expenses are tax-free. Prioritizing HSA contributions can provide significant tax savings while simultaneously building a dedicated fund for healthcare expenses in retirement.

6. Roth IRA: After addressing immediate financial needs and taking advantage of employer-sponsored retirement plans, allocating funds towards a Roth IRA can further enhance your retirement readiness. Roth IRAs offer tax-free growth and withdrawals in retirement, making them an attractive option for long-term wealth accumulation. Maximize your contributions to a Roth IRA to capitalize on tax-efficient growth opportunities and diversify your retirement savings.

7. Brokerage/Max out 401k/529: Finally, once you've optimized contributions to tax-advantaged accounts and addressed other financial priorities, consider directing additional funds towards taxable brokerage accounts or maximizing contributions to your 401(k) plan. If you have children or are saving for education expenses, funding a 529 college savings plan can provide tax advantages while helping you achieve your education savings goals.

Setting Investment Goals:

Setting clear and achievable investment goals is the foundation of building wealth through investments. Your investment goals should be specific, measurable, achievable, relevant, and time-bound (SMART). Here's how to set effective investment goals:

1. Define Your Objectives:

Start by defining your investment objectives. Are you saving for retirement, purchasing a home, funding education expenses, or building a nest egg for the future? Identifying your goals will help you tailor your investment strategy to meet your specific needs and aspirations.

2. Quantify Your Goals:

Determine how much money you need to achieve each investment goal. Break down your goals into smaller, manageable milestones, and assign a target amount and deadline to each one. Quantifying your goals provides clarity and helps you track your progress over time.

3. Assess Your Risk Tolerance:
Consider your risk tolerance and investment horizon when setting investment goals. Are you comfortable with market fluctuations and volatility, or do you prefer more conservative investments? Understanding your risk tolerance will guide your asset allocation and investment decisions.

4. Prioritize Your Goals:
Rank your investment goals based on their importance and urgency. Focus on high-priority goals first, such as retirement savings or debt repayment, before allocating resources to lower-priority goals. By prioritizing your goals, you can allocate resources more effectively and stay focused on what matters most.

Creating a Diversified Portfolio:

A diversified portfolio is essential for building wealth and mitigating risk. Diversification involves spreading your investments across different asset classes, industries, and geographic regions to reduce the impact of market volatility and fluctuations. Here's how to create a diversified portfolio:

Asset Allocation:
Determine your asset allocation based on your investment goals, risk tolerance, and time horizon. Allocate your portfolio across different asset classes, such as stocks, bonds, cash, and real estate, in proportions that reflect your risk-return profile.

Consider the historical performance, correlation, and risk characteristics of each asset class when determining your asset allocation. Adjust your allocation over time as your financial situation and investment goals evolve.

Stock Sector and Geographic Diversification:
Diversify your stock holdings across different sectors of the economy, such as technology, healthcare, consumer goods, and financials. Avoid overconcentration in any single sector to reduce sector-specific risk.

Additionally, diversify your investments geographically by including international stocks and bonds in your portfolio. Investing in foreign markets provides exposure to different economies, currencies, and geopolitical factors, enhancing portfolio diversification.

Use of Investment Vehicles:
Utilize a mix of investment vehicles, such as mutual funds, exchange-traded funds (ETFs), and individual securities, to achieve diversification. Mutual funds and ETFs offer diversified exposure to multiple assets within a single investment, making them convenient options for individual investors.

Consider including alternative investments, such as real estate investment trusts (REITs), commodities, and private equity, to further diversify your portfolio and access unique sources of returns.

Harnessing the Power of Compounding:

"Compound interest is the eighth wonder of the world. He who understands it, earns it ... he who doesn't ... pays it." – Albert Einstein

Compounding is a powerful wealth-building principle that allows your investment returns to generate additional returns over time. The earlier you start investing and the longer you stay invested, the more significant the impact of compounding on your wealth. Here's how to harness the power of compounding:

1. Start Early and Invest Regularly:
Time is one of the most critical factors in compounding. Start investing as early as possible and contribute regularly to take advantage of the exponential growth of compound returns. Even small, consistent investments can grow significantly over time thanks to compounding.

Set up automatic contributions to your investment accounts, such as a 401(k) or IRA, to ensure consistent and disciplined investing. You can start with as little as $50 a month and with time this can grow to a significant amount of money.

2. Reinvest Dividends and Capital Gains:
Reinvesting dividends and capital gains allows your investment returns to generate additional returns over time. Instead of withdrawing cash distributions, reinvest them back into your portfolio to accelerate wealth accumulation.

Many investment vehicles, such as mutual funds and ETFs, offer dividend reinvestment programs (DRIPs) that automatically reinvest dividends to purchase additional shares of the fund.

Navigating Market Volatility:

Market volatility is a natural part of investing, but it can be unsettling for investors, especially during periods of economic uncertainty or financial turmoil. Here are some strategies for navigating market volatility and staying focused on your long-term investment goals:

1. Maintain a Long-Term Perspective:
Focus on your long-term investment goals and resist the urge to react impulsively to short-term market fluctuations. Market volatility is temporary, but the power of compounding and time in the market can generate significant returns over the long term. Remember you are investing not day trading.

Remember that market downturns present buying opportunities for long-term investors. Instead of panicking, consider taking advantage of lower prices to add to your investment positions and rebalance your portfolio. You can always store additional cash in your investment account and when investment drop buys the asset at a lower price. Make sure you believe in your asset and are confident the price will increase again in time.

2. Stay Diversified and Rebalance Regularly:
Maintain a diversified portfolio across different asset classes and geographic regions to reduce the impact of market volatility on your investments. Regularly review and rebalance your portfolio to ensure that your asset allocation remains aligned with your investment goals and risk tolerance.

Rebalancing involves selling investments that have appreciated in value and reallocating the proceeds into underperforming assets to restore your target asset allocation. Rebalancing helps control risk and maintain portfolio stability during periods of market volatility.

3. Dollar-Cost Averaging:
Dollar-cost averaging (DCA) involves investing a fixed amount of money at regular intervals, regardless of market conditions. DCA allows you to buy more shares when prices are low and fewer shares when prices are high, smoothing out market volatility over time.

Implementing a systematic investment plan, such as investing a fixed amount of money from each paycheck or making regular contributions to your investment accounts, can help you take advantage of DCA and reduce the impact of market fluctuations on your portfolio.

Tax Efficient Investing

Tax-efficient investing strategies are essential for maximizing your after-tax returns and minimizing the impact of taxes on your investment portfolio. By implementing tax-efficient strategies, you can optimize your investment returns and retain more of your investment gains. Here are some tax-efficient investing strategies to consider:

1. Utilize Tax-Advantaged Accounts:
Take advantage of tax-advantaged retirement accounts, such as 401(k)s, IRAs (Traditional and Roth), and Health Savings Accounts (HSAs). Contributions to these accounts may be tax-deductible (for Traditional IRAs and 401(k)s) or tax-free (for Roth IRAs and HSAs), and investment earnings grow tax-deferred or tax-free.

Maximize your contributions to these accounts each year to benefit from tax advantages and accelerate your retirement savings. Consider contributing the maximum allowable amount to your employer-sponsored 401(k) plan and contributing to IRAs or HSAs if eligible.

2. Tax-Loss Harvesting:
Tax-loss harvesting involves strategically selling investments that have experienced losses to offset capital gains and reduce your tax liability. By realizing losses, you can offset gains in other investments or up to $3,000 in ordinary income per year ($1,500 for married individuals filing separately).
Reinvest the proceeds from the sale into similar, but not identical, investments to maintain your portfolio's desired asset allocation while capturing the tax benefits of realizing losses.

3. Asset Location:
Asset location refers to strategically placing different types of investments in taxable and tax-advantaged accounts to maximize after-tax returns. Generally, tax-efficient investments, such as index funds, ETFs, and tax-exempt bonds, are held in taxable accounts, while tax-inefficient investments, such as actively managed funds and high-yield bonds, are held in tax-advantaged accounts.
By allocating tax-efficient investments to taxable accounts and tax-inefficient investments to tax-advantaged accounts, you can minimize the tax impact on your investment returns and optimize after-tax performance.

4. Dividend Reinvestment:
If you receive dividends from your investments, consider reinvesting them through a dividend reinvestment plan (DRIP) or automatic dividend reinvestment program. Reinvesting dividends allows you to purchase additional shares of the same investment without incurring transaction costs, effectively compounding your returns over time.
Alternatively, if you're in a high tax bracket or prefer to receive income in cash, you may choose to direct dividends to a cash account to avoid immediate tax consequences.

5. Tax-Efficient Investments:

Invest in tax-efficient investment vehicles, such as index funds, ETFs, and municipal bonds, which tend to generate fewer taxable distributions compared to actively managed funds or individual stocks. Index funds and ETFs typically have lower turnover and capital gains distributions, resulting in lower tax liabilities for investors.

Municipal bonds offer tax-exempt interest income at the federal level and may also be exempt from state and local taxes if issued within your state of residence. Consider allocating a portion of your fixed-income investments to municipal bonds to minimize tax exposure and enhance after-tax returns.

6. Long-Term Investing:

Long-term investing can result in lower tax rates on investment gains compared to short-term investing. Investments held for more than one year qualify for long-term capital gains tax rates, which are generally lower than ordinary income tax rates.

Consider adopting a buy-and-hold investment strategy and holding investments for the long term to benefit from favorable capital gains tax treatment. Avoid frequent trading or short-term speculation, which can trigger higher tax liabilities and erode investment returns.

7. Tax-Efficient Withdrawal Strategies:

Develop tax-efficient withdrawal strategies in retirement to minimize the tax impact on your income and investment distributions. Coordinate withdrawals from different types of accounts, such as taxable, tax-deferred, and tax-free accounts, to manage your tax bracket and optimize after-tax income.

Consider strategies such as Roth IRA conversions, which allow you to convert traditional IRA assets to Roth IRAs and pay taxes upfront at potentially lower rates. Roth IRA withdrawals in retirement are tax-free, providing tax diversification and flexibility in managing your retirement income.

By implementing these tax-efficient investing strategies, you can minimize the impact of taxes on your investment returns and maximize after-tax wealth accumulation. Consult with a qualified financial advisor or tax professional to develop a personalized tax-efficient investment plan tailored to your individual financial situation, goals, and risk tolerance. Regularly review and adjust your investment strategy to adapt to changes in tax laws, market conditions, and your financial objectives.

Conclusion:

Building wealth through investments requires careful planning, disciplined investing, and a long-term perspective. By setting clear investment goals, creating a diversified portfolio, harnessing the power of compounding, and navigating market volatility effectively, you can grow your wealth over time and achieve financial independence. Remember, investing is a journey, not a destination, and success requires patience, persistence, and a commitment to your financial goals. Start investing early, stay diversified, and stay focused on the long term, and you'll be well on your way to building wealth and securing your financial future.

CHAPTER 6: PROTECTING YOUR FINANCES

Protecting your finances is crucial for achieving financial security and peace of mind. In this chapter, we'll explore various strategies and tools for safeguarding your financial well-being, including the importance of insurance, estate planning basics, understanding risk management, and safeguarding against identity theft and fraud.

Importance of Insurance:

Insurance plays a critical role in protecting your finances from unforeseen events and risks. By transferring the financial risk to an insurance company, you can mitigate potential losses and ensure that you and your loved ones are financially protected. Here are some essential types of insurance to consider:

Health Insurance:
Health insurance covers medical expenses and provides financial protection against illness, injury, and medical emergencies. It helps pay for doctor visits, hospitalization, prescription medications, and other healthcare services.
Having health insurance can prevent medical bills from depleting your savings or causing financial hardship. Make sure to review your health insurance coverage regularly and choose a plan that meets your needs and budget.

Life Insurance:
Life insurance provides financial protection to your loved ones in the event of your death. It pays out a death benefit to your beneficiaries, which can be used to replace lost income, pay off

debts, cover funeral expenses, or fund future expenses.
Consider purchasing life insurance if you have dependents who rely on your income, such as a spouse, children, or aging parents. Choose between term life insurance, which provides coverage for a specific period, or permanent life insurance, which offers coverage for your lifetime.

Disability Insurance:
Disability insurance replaces a portion of your income if you're unable to work due to illness or injury. It provides financial protection against the loss of income and helps cover essential expenses, such as mortgage or rent payments, utilities, and groceries.
Disability insurance is especially important for individuals who rely on their income to support themselves and their families. Make sure to understand the terms and coverage limits of your disability insurance policy to ensure adequate protection.

Homeowners Insurance:
Homeowners insurance protects your home and personal belongings against damage or loss caused by perils such as fire, theft, vandalism, and natural disasters. It also provides liability coverage in case someone is injured on your property and sues you for damages.
Homeowners insurance is typically required by mortgage lenders and provides essential financial protection for one of your most significant assets. Review your policy regularly to ensure that you have adequate coverage for your home and belongings.

Auto Insurance:
Auto insurance covers damages and liabilities associated with owning and operating a vehicle. It provides financial protection against accidents, theft, vandalism, and other unforeseen events on the road.
Auto insurance is mandatory in most states and helps cover repair costs, medical expenses, and legal fees in case of an accident. Choose a policy that meets your state's minimum requirements

and provides adequate coverage for your vehicle and personal liability.

Estate Planning Basics:

Estate planning is the process of arranging your affairs and assets to ensure that your wishes are carried out in the event of your death or incapacity. It involves creating essential legal documents, such as wills, trusts, and powers of attorney, to protect your assets and provide for your loved ones. Here are some estate planning basics to consider:

Wills:
A will is a legal document that outlines how you want your assets to be distributed after your death. It allows you to designate beneficiaries for your property, appoint guardians for minor children, and specify any funeral or burial instructions.

Having a will is essential for ensuring that your assets are distributed according to your wishes and minimizing the risk of family disputes or legal challenges. Update your will regularly to reflect changes in your family, finances, or estate planning goals.

Trusts:
A trust is a legal arrangement that allows you to transfer assets to a trustee who manages them on behalf of beneficiaries. Trusts provide flexibility, control, and privacy in managing your assets and distributing them to your heirs.

Consider establishing a trust to protect assets, minimize estate taxes, or provide for specific needs of beneficiaries, such as minor children, individuals with special needs, or charitable organizations. Consult with an estate planning attorney to determine the type of trust that best meets your needs.

Powers of Attorney:
A power of attorney is a legal document that authorizes someone to act on your behalf in financial or medical matters if you become incapacitated. It allows a trusted individual, known as an agent or attorney-in-fact, to make decisions and manage your affairs when

you're unable to do so.

Create both a financial power of attorney and a healthcare power of attorney to ensure that your interests are protected in case of incapacity. Choose someone you trust implicitly to act as your agent and make decisions that align with your wishes.

Will vs. Trust

A will and a trust are both estate planning tools that allow individuals to dictate how their assets will be distributed after their death, but they serve different purposes and offer distinct advantages. Here are the key differences between a will and a trust:

1. Function:

Will: A will is a legal document that outlines how a person's assets will be distributed upon their death. It allows individuals to specify beneficiaries for their property, appoint guardians for minor children, name an executor to oversee the distribution of assets, and designate any final wishes or instructions.

Trust: A trust is a legal arrangement that allows a trustee to hold assets on behalf of beneficiaries according to the terms specified in the trust document. Trusts can be used to manage and distribute assets during the grantor's lifetime and after their death, providing greater control and flexibility over the disposition of assets.

2. Probate:

Will: Assets distributed through a will must go through the probate process, which is a court-supervised proceeding to validate the will, settle debts, and distribute assets to beneficiaries. Probate can be time-consuming, expensive, and subject to public scrutiny, potentially delaying the distribution of assets to heirs.

Trust: Assets held in a trust typically bypass the probate process, as they are owned by the trust and managed by the trustee. Upon the grantor's death, the trustee can distribute assets to beneficiaries according to the terms of the trust without court involvement, providing privacy, efficiency, and cost savings.

3. Privacy:

Will: Wills are public documents once they are probated, meaning that the contents of the will, including assets and beneficiaries, become part of the public record. Anyone can request access to probate court records and obtain information about the deceased person's estate.

Trust: Trusts offer greater privacy compared to wills because they are not subject to probate and do not become part of the public record. The terms of the trust and the identities of beneficiaries remain private, providing confidentiality and discretion in estate planning.

4. Flexibility and Control:

Will: Wills provide a straightforward method for distributing assets after death, but they offer limited flexibility and control over how assets are managed and distributed. The instructions in a will are binding, but they are subject to interpretation by the probate court and may be challenged by disgruntled heirs.

Trust: Trusts offer greater flexibility and control over the management and distribution of assets. Trust documents can specify detailed instructions for managing assets, such as conditions for distributions, timing of payments, and appointment of successor trustees. Trusts can also be used to protect assets from creditors, ensure ongoing financial support for beneficiaries, and minimize taxes.

5. Lifetime Planning:

Will: Wills only take effect upon the death of the individual, providing instructions for the distribution of assets after death.

They do not govern the management or disposition of assets during the individual's lifetime.

Trust: Trusts can be established during the grantor's lifetime and used to manage assets during their lifetime and after their death. Living trusts, also known as revocable trusts, allow individuals to retain control over their assets while specifying how they should be managed and distributed both during their lifetime and upon their death.

In summary, while both wills and trusts are essential estate planning tools, they serve different purposes and offer different benefits. Wills provide instructions for the distribution of assets after death and are subject to probate, while trusts offer greater control, privacy, and flexibility over the management and distribution of assets both during lifetime and after death. Depending on your individual circumstances and estate planning goals, you may choose to use a will, a trust, or a combination of both to ensure that your wishes are carried out and your assets are protected for future generations. It's essential to consult with an experienced estate planning attorney to determine the best approach for your specific needs and objectives.

Understanding Risk Management:

Risk management involves identifying, assessing, and mitigating risks that could jeopardize your financial well-being. It's essential to understand various types of risks and implement strategies to manage them effectively. Here are some key principles of risk management:

Identify Risks:
Identify potential risks that could impact your finances, such as market risk, inflation risk, longevity risk, and liquidity risk. Assess the likelihood and potential impact of each risk on your financial goals and develop strategies to mitigate them.

Diversification:

Diversification is a risk management strategy that involves spreading your investments across different asset classes, industries, and geographic regions. By diversifying your portfolio, you can reduce the impact of individual risks and enhance overall portfolio stability.

Allocate your investments among stocks, bonds, cash equivalents, and alternative assets to achieve diversification and manage risk effectively. Regularly rebalance your portfolio to maintain the desired asset allocation and risk level.

Insurance:
Insurance is an essential tool for managing various types of risks, including health, life, disability, home, and auto risks. Purchase insurance policies that provide adequate coverage for potential losses and liabilities and review them regularly to ensure that your coverage remains up to date.

Emergency Fund:
Maintain an emergency fund to cover unexpected expenses or financial emergencies, such as medical bills, car repairs, or job loss. Aim to save three to six months' worth of living expenses in a liquid, easily accessible account, such as a savings account or money market fund.

This is one of the best and most important things to have when starting your journey in personal finance.

Safeguarding Against Identity Theft and Fraud:

Identity theft and fraud are significant threats to your financial security and can result in financial losses, damaged credit, and emotional stress. Protect yourself against identity theft and fraud by implementing the following measures:

Monitor Your Accounts:
Regularly monitor your bank accounts, credit card statements, and financial transactions for any unauthorized or suspicious activity. Review account statements promptly and report any discrepancies or fraudulent charges to your financial institution.

Secure Personal Information:
Safeguard your personal information, such as social security number, date of birth, and financial account numbers, from theft or unauthorized access. Be cautious when sharing sensitive information online or over the phone, and only provide it to trusted sources.

Use Strong Passwords and Security Measures:
Use strong, unique passwords for online accounts and regularly update them to prevent unauthorized access. Enable two-factor authentication (2FA) or multi-factor authentication (MFA) for added security and avoid using public Wi-Fi networks for sensitive transactions.

Shred Sensitive Documents:
Shred or securely dispose of documents containing personal or financial information, such as bank statements, credit card offers, and receipts. Use a cross-cut shredder to destroy documents thoroughly and prevent identity thieves from accessing your information.

Be Vigilant Against Phishing Scams:
Be wary of unsolicited emails, phone calls, or text messages requesting personal or financial information. Do not click on links or download attachments from unknown or suspicious sources, as they may be phishing attempts to steal your information.

Conclusion:

Protecting your finances is essential for achieving financial security and peace of mind. By understanding the importance of insurance, implementing estate planning basics, managing risk effectively, and safeguarding against identity theft and fraud, you can mitigate potential threats to your financial well-being and build a solid foundation for your future. Take proactive steps to protect yourself and your loved ones, and regularly review and update your financial protection strategies to adapt to changes in your circumstances or the external environment. With careful planning and diligence, you can safeguard your finances and achieve your long-term financial goals.

CHAPTER 7: BUILDING MULTIPLE STREAMS OF INCOME

In today's dynamic and uncertain economy, relying solely on a single source of income may not provide the financial security and stability needed to achieve your long-term goals. Building multiple streams of income can diversify your earnings, increase your financial resilience, and create opportunities for wealth accumulation. In this chapter, we'll explore various strategies for building multiple streams of income, including passive income opportunities, starting a side business or freelancing gig, investing in income-generating assets, and maximizing your earning potential.

Exploring Passive Income Opportunities:

Passive income refers to earnings generated with minimal effort or active involvement on your part. Unlike traditional employment income, which requires your time and labor, passive income streams can provide ongoing revenue streams with less direct effort once set up. Here are some passive income opportunities to consider:

Rental Income:
Owning rental properties and leasing them to tenants can generate passive rental income. Real estate investments, such as residential homes, commercial properties, or vacation rentals, can provide steady cash flow and potential long-term appreciation. Consider leveraging rental properties through financing options

such as mortgages to increase your purchasing power and enhance returns. Property management services can help alleviate the day-to-day responsibilities of managing rental properties.

Dividend Stocks:
Investing in dividend-paying stocks allows you to earn passive income through regular dividend distributions. Dividend stocks are shares of publicly traded companies that distribute a portion of their profits to shareholders in the form of dividends.

Focus on established companies with a history of consistent dividend payments and sustainable dividend yields. Reinvesting dividends through dividend reinvestment plans (DRIPs) can compound your returns over time and accelerate wealth accumulation.

Interest-Bearing Investments:
Interest-bearing investments, such as bonds, certificates of deposit (CDs), and high-yield savings accounts, can provide passive income in the form of interest payments. These investments offer predictable income streams and are relatively low risk compared to equity investments.

Diversify your fixed-income portfolio across different types of bonds and maturities to manage interest rate risk and maximize yield potential. Consider laddering bonds with staggered maturities to balance liquidity and yield.

Peer-to-Peer Lending:
Peer-to-peer (P2P) lending platforms allow individuals to lend money to borrowers in exchange for interest payments. P2P lending facilitates direct lending between investors and borrowers, bypassing traditional financial institutions.

Research P2P lending platforms carefully and assess borrower risk profiles, loan terms, and default rates before investing. Diversify your P2P lending portfolio across multiple loans to mitigate default risk and enhance overall returns.

Start a Side Business or Freelancing Gig:

Starting a side business or freelancing gig is an excellent way to generate additional income outside of your primary job or career. Whether you have a passion project, specialized skills, or entrepreneurial aspirations, launching a side hustle can provide extra income and potentially grow into a full-fledged business. Here's how to get started:

1. Identify Your Skills and Interests:

Assess your skills, expertise, and interests to identify potential business opportunities or freelance services. Consider your hobbies, talents, and professional experience that you can leverage to create value for others.

Explore niche markets or areas of high demand where your skills or expertise can fill a gap or solve a problem. Conduct market research to validate your business idea and assess the competitive landscape.

2. Create a Business Plan:

Develop a comprehensive business plan outlining your business concept, target market, value proposition, competitive analysis, marketing strategy, and financial projections. A well-thought-out business plan will serve as a roadmap for your business and guide decision-making.

Define your business goals, objectives, and milestones, and establish measurable targets to track progress and success. Consider seeking feedback from mentors, advisors, or industry experts to refine your business plan and identify potential challenges.

3. Start Small and Scale Over Time:

Begin by testing your business idea on a small scale to minimize risk and validate market demand. Launch a pilot program, offer beta testing, or provide sample services to gauge customer interest and gather feedback.

As you gain traction and confidence in your business, gradually scale up operations and expand your offerings. Invest in marketing, branding, and customer acquisition strategies to attract and retain clients or customers.

4. Manage Your Time and Resources:
Balancing a side business or freelancing gig with your primary job and other commitments requires effective time management and resource allocation. Prioritize tasks, set realistic deadlines, and establish boundaries to avoid burnout and maintain work-life balance.

Allocate resources wisely and focus on activities that generate the highest return on investment (ROI) for your business. Outsource non-core functions or delegate tasks to freelancers or virtual assistants to free up your time and focus on revenue-generating activities.

Investing in Income-Generating Assets:

Investing in income-generating assets can provide passive income streams and build wealth over time. Income-generating assets are assets that produce regular cash flow or dividends, allowing you to earn income while preserving or growing your capital. Here are some income-generating assets to consider:

Real Estate Investment Trusts (REITs):
REITs are publicly traded companies that own and operate income-producing real estate properties, such as office buildings, shopping malls, apartments, and hotels. Investing in REITs allows you to earn rental income and potential capital appreciation without directly owning physical properties.

Choose REITs with diversified portfolios, strong track records of income distribution, and competitive yields. Consider investing in different types of REITs, such as equity REITs, mortgage REITs, and hybrid REITs, to diversify risk and enhance returns.

Master Limited Partnerships (MLPs):
MLPs are publicly traded partnerships that own and operate energy infrastructure assets, such as pipelines, storage terminals,

and processing facilities. MLPs generate income from the transportation, storage, and processing of oil, natural gas, and other energy commodities.

MLPs typically distribute a significant portion of their income to investors in the form of tax-advantaged distributions known as distributions. Invest in MLPs with stable cash flows, strong management teams, and attractive distribution yields to generate passive income and potentially benefit from capital appreciation.

High-Dividend Stocks:

High-dividend stocks are shares of companies that pay above-average dividends relative to their stock price. These companies often have stable cash flows, strong balance sheets, and a history of consistent dividend payments.

Look for high-dividend stocks with sustainable dividend yields, low payout ratios, and a track record of dividend growth. Focus on companies in defensive sectors, such as utilities, consumer staples, and healthcare, which are less sensitive to economic cycles and market volatility.

Be careful as a high yield can also mean less capital appreciation.

Annuities:

Annuities are financial products offered by insurance companies that provide regular payments to investors over a specified period or for the rest of their lives. Annuities can offer guaranteed income streams, tax-deferred growth, and protection against longevity risk.

Consider purchasing immediate annuities or deferred annuities to supplement retirement income, cover essential expenses, or provide financial security in later years. Compare different types of annuities, such as fixed annuities, variable annuities, and indexed annuities, to find the best fit for your financial needs and objectives.

Maximizing Your Earning Potential:

Maximizing your earning potential involves identifying opportunities to increase your income, enhance your skills and qualifications, and leverage your resources effectively. Whether through advancing your career, pursuing education and training, or developing additional sources of income, maximizing your earning potential can help you achieve your financial goals faster and more efficiently. Here are some strategies to consider:

Invest in Education and Skills Development:
Continuously invest in your education, skills, and professional development to stay competitive in the job market and increase your earning potential. Pursue certifications, advanced degrees, or specialized training programs that align with your career goals and interests.

Stay informed about industry trends, emerging technologies, and market demand for specific skills. Seek opportunities for continuous learning and skill acquisition to enhance your value proposition to employers or clients.

Negotiate Your Salary and Benefits:
Advocate for yourself and negotiate your salary, bonuses, and benefits during job interviews, performance reviews, or job transitions. Research industry benchmarks, salary surveys, and compensation data to support your negotiation efforts and ensure fair compensation.

Highlight your accomplishments, contributions, and unique skills when discussing compensation with employers. Be prepared to negotiate non-monetary benefits, such as flexible work arrangements, professional development opportunities, and performance incentives.

Create Multiple Income Streams:
Diversify your income sources by creating multiple streams of income through side hustles, freelancing gigs, investments, or passive income opportunities. Explore different income-generating activities that align with your interests, skills, and resources.

Build scalable and sustainable income streams that complement your primary source of income and provide financial stability and flexibility. Leverage technology, automation, and outsourcing to streamline operations and maximize efficiency in managing multiple income streams.

Network and Build Relationships:
Cultivate professional relationships, expand your network, and build connections with industry peers, mentors, and influencers. Networking can open doors to new opportunities, job leads, and potential collaborations that can enhance your earning potential. Attend industry events, conferences, and networking groups to meet like-minded professionals and exchange ideas and experiences. Engage in online networking through social media platforms, professional associations, and virtual communities to expand your reach and visibility in your field.

50 easy passive income side hustles that you can consider:

1. Dividend Stocks: Invest in dividend-paying stocks that provide regular income through dividend distributions.

2. High-Yield Savings Accounts: Open a high-yield savings account with a competitive interest rate to earn passive income on your savings.

3. Peer-to-Peer Lending: Invest in peer-to-peer lending platforms to lend money to borrowers and earn interest on your investments.

4. Real Estate Crowdfunding: Participate in real estate crowdfunding platforms to invest in real estate projects and earn rental income or capital appreciation.

5. REITs (Real Estate Investment Trusts): Invest in publicly traded REITs that own and operate income-generating real estate properties.

6. Dividend ETFs (Exchange-Traded Funds): Invest in dividend-focused ETFs that hold a diversified portfolio of dividend-paying

stocks.

7. Robo-Advisors: Use robo-advisors to automate your investment portfolio management and earn passive returns through diversified investments.

8. Online Courses: Create and sell online courses on platforms like Udemy or Teachable to generate passive income from course sales.

9. Ebooks: Write and self-publish ebooks on platforms like Amazon Kindle Direct Publishing to earn royalties on book sales.

10. Print-on-Demand Products: Design and sell print-on-demand products, such as t-shirts, mugs, and phone cases, on platforms like Printful or Redbubble.

11. Affiliate Marketing: Promote affiliate products or services on your blog, website, or social media channels and earn commissions for referred sales.

12. YouTube Channel: Start a YouTube channel and monetize it through advertising revenue, sponsored content, and affiliate marketing.

13. Podcasting: Create a podcast and monetize it through sponsorships, advertising, and listener donations.

14. Membership Sites: Create a membership site or subscription service offering premium content, courses, or resources for a monthly fee.

15. Dropshipping: Set up an online store and use dropshipping to sell products without holding inventory or shipping items yourself.

16. Stock Photography: License your photos to stock photography websites and earn royalties whenever someone downloads or purchases your images.

17. Digital Products: Create and sell digital products, such as templates, printables, or software, on platforms like Etsy or

Gumroad.

18. Rental Property: Purchase rental properties and earn passive income from rental payments after covering expenses like mortgage, taxes, and maintenance.

19. Airbnb Hosting: Rent out a spare room or property on Airbnb and earn passive income from short-term rentals.

20. Vending Machines: Invest in vending machines and earn passive income from sales of snacks, beverages, or other items.

21. Laundry Services: Start a laundry pickup and delivery service or invest in laundry machines and earn passive income from service fees or machine usage.

22. Car Rental: Rent out your car through platforms like Turo or Getaround and earn passive income from rental fees.

23. Storage Rentals: Rent out storage space in your garage, basement, or attic and earn passive income from storage fees.

24. Parking Rentals: Rent out parking spaces or driveways in high-demand areas and earn passive income from parking fees.

25. ATM Ownership: Invest in ATMs and earn passive income from transaction fees charged to users.

26. Bookkeeping Services: Offer bookkeeping or accounting services to small businesses and earn passive income from monthly retainer fees.

27. Virtual Assistant Services: Provide virtual assistant services, such as administrative support, email management, or social media management, and earn passive income on a freelance basis.

28. Printables Shop: Create and sell printable planners, organizers, or artwork on Etsy or your own online store.

29. Affiliate Blogs: Start a niche blog and monetize it through affiliate marketing, sponsored content, and display advertising.

30. Pet Sitting or Dog Walking: Offer pet sitting or dog walking services in your local area and earn passive income from pet care fees.

31. House Sitting: Offer house sitting services to homeowners while they're away on vacation or business trips and earn passive income from house sitting fees.

32. Tutoring Services: Offer tutoring services in subjects like math, science, or languages and earn passive income from hourly tutoring fees.

33. Music Lessons: Offer music lessons in-person or online and earn passive income from lesson fees.

34. Fitness Training: Offer personal training or fitness coaching services in-person or online and earn passive income from training fees.

35. Meal Prep Services: Offer meal prep or cooking services to busy individuals or families and earn passive income from meal delivery or service fees.

36. Consulting Services: Offer consulting services in your area of expertise, such as business, marketing, or technology, and earn passive income from consulting fees.

37. Event Planning: Offer event planning or coordination services for weddings, parties, or corporate events and earn passive income from event fees.

38. Property Management: Offer property management services to landlords or real estate investors and earn passive income from management fees.

39. Language Translation Services: Offer language translation or interpretation services and earn passive income from translation fees.

40. Graphic Design Services: Offer graphic design services, such as

logo design, branding, or marketing materials, and earn passive income from design fees.

41. Web Design Services: Offer web design or development services and earn passive income from website creation or maintenance fees.

42. Social Media Management: Offer social media management services to businesses or individuals and earn passive income from management fees.

43. Copywriting Services: Offer copywriting or content writing services and earn passive income from writing fees.

44. Editing and Proofreading Services: Offer editing and proofreading services for written content and earn passive income from editing fees.

45. Transcription Services: Offer transcription services for audio or video recordings and earn passive income from transcription fees.

46. Remote Tech Support: Offer remote tech support or IT services to businesses or individuals and earn passive income from support fees.

47. Data Entry Services: Offer data entry or data processing services and earn passive income from data entry fees.

48. Drop Servicing: Act as a middleman between clients and service providers, outsourcing tasks or projects and earning passive income from service fees.

49. Language Teaching: Teach languages online through platforms like Italki or Verbling and earn passive income from teaching fees.

50. Survey Taking: Take online surveys or participate in market research studies and earn passive income from survey payouts or rewards.

These passive income side hustles offer opportunities to earn additional income with varying levels of time commitment and investment. Choose the ones that align with your skills, interests, and resources, and consider diversifying your income streams for greater financial stability and flexibility. Remember to research each opportunity thoroughly, assess potential risks and rewards, and adapt your strategy based on your goals and circumstances. With dedication and perseverance, you can build multiple streams of passive income and achieve your financial objectives.

Conclusion:

Building multiple streams of income is a powerful strategy for achieving financial security, diversifying risk, and accelerating wealth accumulation. Whether through passive income opportunities, side businesses or freelancing gigs, income-generating assets, or maximizing your earning potential, there are numerous ways to create additional sources of income and achieve your financial goals. Take proactive steps to explore and pursue income-generating opportunities that align with your skills, interests, and financial objectives. Continuously evaluate and adjust your income streams to adapt to changing market conditions, economic trends, and personal circumstances. With perseverance, creativity, and strategic planning, you can build a robust portfolio of income streams that provide financial independence, freedom, and peace of mind for the future.

CHAPTER 8: PLANNING FOR MAJOR FINANCIAL MILESTONES

Life unfolds through a series of significant milestones, each presenting unique opportunities and challenges. These milestones often come with substantial financial implications, requiring careful planning and preparation. In this chapter, we will delve into the intricacies of planning for some of the most common major financial milestones: saving for education, buying a home, getting married, and starting a family. By understanding the financial aspects of these life events, you can navigate them confidently and set yourself up for success.

Saving for Education:

Investing in education is an investment in the future, whether it's for your own advancement or that of your children. The rising costs of higher education necessitate proactive planning. Here are some strategies for saving for education:

College Funds:
Open a dedicated college savings account, such as a 529 plan or Coverdell Education Savings Account (ESA), as early as possible. These accounts offer tax advantages and flexible investment options tailored to educational expenses.

Regular Contributions:
Commit to making regular contributions to your college savings accounts, even if they are modest. Consistent saving over time can significantly impact the growth of your education fund and

alleviate the burden of future tuition expenses.

529 Plan

A 529 plan is a tax-advantaged savings plan designed to encourage saving for future education costs. Named after Section 529 of the Internal Revenue Code, these plans are sponsored by states, state agencies, or educational institutions and are authorized by Congress. Here's how they typically work:

1. Types of 529 Plans: There are two main types of 529 plans: prepaid tuition plans and education savings plans.

   - Prepaid Tuition Plans: These plans allow you to prepay tuition expenses at eligible colleges and universities. They may also allow for the prepayment of mandatory fees and sometimes room and board. The value of the plan typically rises with the cost of tuition. These plans are usually sponsored by state governments and have residency requirements.

   - Education Savings Plans: Education savings plans operate like a tax-advantaged investment account, where you can contribute money to be invested in a variety of mutual funds or similar investments. The funds can be used for qualified education expenses at any eligible educational institution, including colleges, universities, vocational schools, and even some foreign institutions.

2. Tax Advantages: The earnings in a 529 plan grow tax-deferred, meaning you don't have to pay federal taxes on the investment gains as long as the money is used for qualified education expenses. Additionally, some states offer tax deductions or credits for contributions made to their 529 plans.

3. Qualified Education Expenses: Funds from a 529 plan can be used for a variety of qualified education expenses, including tuition, fees, books, supplies, equipment, and in some cases, room and board. Starting in 2019, up to $10,000 per year per beneficiary can also be used for K-12 tuition expenses.

4. Flexibility: 529 plans offer flexibility in terms of the choice of beneficiary. If the intended beneficiary doesn't use all the funds or decides not to pursue higher education, you can change the beneficiary to another family member without incurring penalties (as long as they are a qualified family member).
Starting in 2024 you can roll unused 529 assets into the account beneficiaries Roth IRA up to a lifetime limit of $35,000.

5. Contributions and Limits: While contribution limits vary by state, they are typically quite high, often in the hundreds of thousands of dollars. Contributions to a 529 plan are considered gifts for tax purposes, and thus there are federal gift tax considerations. However, individuals can contribute up to the gift tax exclusion amount each year without triggering the gift tax ($18,000 per individual in 2024).

6. Investment Options: Education savings plans typically offer a range of investment options, allowing you to choose an investment strategy that suits your risk tolerance and investment goals. These options can include age-based portfolios, which automatically adjust to become more conservative as the beneficiary approaches college age, as well as static investment options.

Overall, 529 plans can be powerful tools for families looking to save for education expenses while benefiting from tax advantages and investment growth potential. However, it's essential to carefully consider the specific features and fees associated with the plan you choose, as well as any potential impacts on financial aid eligibility.

Buying a Home:

Owning a home is a cornerstone of the American dream, but it requires careful financial planning to achieve. Here's how to prepare for the homebuying process:

Mortgages:
Assess your financial readiness for homeownership by evaluating your credit score, debt-to-income ratio, and savings. Shop around for mortgage lenders to find competitive rates and terms that fit your budget and financial goals.

Down Payments:
Start saving for a down payment, aiming to set aside at least 20% of the home's purchase price. While some loan programs allow for lower down payments, a higher down payment can lower your monthly mortgage payments and eliminate the need for private mortgage insurance (PMI).

Though 20% is a nice target, with the rising prices of homes in the US, it is often an impossible dream. Shooting for 5% down payment may be more realistic in today's world.

Home Affordability:
Determine how much house you can afford by considering factors like your income, expenses, and long-term financial goals. Use online affordability calculators and consult with a financial advisor to ensure that homeownership aligns with your overall financial plan.

I like to limit my mortgage to about 25% of my monthly income. This will prevent you from falling into a mortgage trap that so many Americans do and become house poor.

Getting Married:

Marriage is a joyous occasion that marks the beginning of a new chapter in your life. However, merging your finances requires careful consideration and planning. Here's how to navigate the financial aspects of marriage:

Financial Conversations:
Have open and honest conversations with your partner about money, including your financial goals, values, and concerns. Discuss topics like budgeting, saving, debt management, and long-term planning to ensure alignment and transparency.

Picking someone to marry is almost like picking a business partner. If you share the same financial goals and work toward these goals together this will accelerate the rate you achieve your goals and prevent tension and resentment in the marriage.

Joint Finances:
Decide whether to merge your finances completely, keep separate accounts, or adopt a hybrid approach that combines joint and individual accounts. Consider factors like income disparity, spending habits, and financial autonomy when making this decision.
There is a sense of true unity when combining finances. It makes you and your partner feel more like a team and in it together. However, every situation is different and there is nothing wrong with separate finances if it works better for you and your partner.

Starting a Family:

Welcoming a new addition to the family is an exciting and transformative experience, but it also comes with increased financial responsibilities. Here's how to prepare for parenthood financially:

Budgeting for Parenthood:
Create a comprehensive budget that accounts for the additional expenses associated with raising a child, such as childcare, medical costs, diapers, and education savings. Factor in both short-term and long-term expenses to ensure that your budget is realistic and sustainable.

College Savings:
Many families choose to open a 529 plan shortly after the birth of a child or during early childhood. This gives you ample time to contribute regularly and build up savings over many years. Plus, starting early can help distribute the contributions over a longer period, potentially reducing the financial strain.

Emergency Fund:
Build or replenish your emergency fund to cover unexpected

expenses that may arise during pregnancy or after the baby is born. Aim to save three to six months' worth of living expenses in a liquid, easily accessible account to provide financial security and peace of mind.

Estate Planning:
Deciding whether to start a trust or will after the birth of your first child depends on various factors, including your financial situation, estate planning goals, and preferences.

There are both upfront cost and management fees to keep in mind.

I would recommend setting up the trust after your partner and you are finished having children. That way you don't have to pay to change the document after each new member of the family.

Ultimately, whether to start a trust after the birth of your first child is a personal decision. Taking the time to evaluate your options and seek professional advice can ensure that you make the best choice for your family's future.

Conclusion:

Planning for major financial milestones is essential for achieving your goals and navigating life's transitions with confidence. Whether you're saving for education, buying a home, getting married, or starting a family, thoughtful planning and proactive decision-making can set you on the path to financial success. By understanding the financial implications of these milestones and implementing sound strategies, you can build a secure financial foundation for yourself and your loved ones, ensuring a brighter future for years to come.

CHAPTER 9: RETIREMENT PLANNING

Retirement is a significant milestone in life, marking the transition from work to leisure and providing an opportunity to enjoy the fruits of your labor. However, achieving a financially secure retirement requires careful planning and preparation. In this chapter, we will explore the essential aspects of retirement planning, including understanding retirement accounts, estimating your retirement needs, strategies for catching up on retirement savings, and planning for a successful retirement.

Understanding Retirement Accounts:

Retirement accounts are essential tools for building a nest egg to support you during retirement. Understanding the different types of retirement accounts and their features is crucial for effective retirement planning. Here are some common retirement accounts:

401K:

A 401K is an employer-sponsored retirement savings plan offered by many companies to their employees. Contributions to a traditional 401(k) are made on a pre-tax basis, reducing your taxable income in the year of contribution. The earnings on your investments grow tax-deferred until withdrawal, typically in retirement. Which means you pay taxes in retirement on the money earned from your 401K.

Contributions:
Employees can contribute a portion of their pre-tax income to their 401(k) account, up to a certain limit set by the IRS each

year. As of 2024, the contribution limit is $23,000 for individuals under 50 years old, and $30,500 for individuals aged 50 and older (including catch-up contributions).

Company Match:
Many employers offer a Company Match when you contribute to a 401k. This is usually up to a certain percentage of your own contributions. This is essentially free money, and it is advisable to contribute enough money to your 401k to at least to get the full company match.

Investment Options:
Within a 401k, employees typically have a range of mutual funds and target date funds. There is usually not a lot of options to choose from.

Vesting:
Employer contributions to a 401(k) plan may be subject to a vesting schedule, which determines how much of the employer's contributions the employee is entitled to keep if they leave the company before a certain period. Employees are always fully vested in their own contributions.

Withdrawals and penalties:
Withdrawals from a 401(k) are generally subject to income tax, and if taken before the age of 59½, they may also be subject to a 10% early withdrawal penalty, with some exceptions such as hardship withdrawals or qualified distributions for certain purposes like buying a first home or paying for education expenses.

IRA (Individual Retirement Account):
An IRA is a personal retirement savings account that individuals can open and contribute to independently of their employer. Contributions to a traditional IRA may be tax-deductible, depending on your income level and participation in employer-sponsored retirement plans. Similar to a 401(k), earnings in a traditional IRA grow tax-deferred until withdrawal. You pay taxes

for earnings at the time of withdrawal in retirement.

IRAs are personal so there is no company match, or vesting schedules involved.

Contribution limits:

There are annual contribution limits for IRAs set by the IRS. As of 2024, the contribution limit is $7,000 per year for individuals under 50 years old, and $8,000 for individuals aged 50 and older (including catch-up contributions). These limits may change over time due to inflation adjustments.

Investment Options:

IRAs have access to a wide array of investment options. They are only limited by the financial institution where you choose to house your IRA. You can invest in stocks, bonds, mutual funds, exchange-traded funds (ETFs), and other assets.

Withdrawals:

Withdrawals from a traditional IRA are generally subject to income tax, and if taken before the age of 59½, they may also be subject to a 10% early withdrawal penalty, with some exceptions. Withdrawals from a Roth IRA are generally tax-free if they meet certain requirements.

Roth IRA:

A Roth IRA is another type of individual retirement account that offers tax advantages. Contributions to a Roth IRA are made with after-tax dollars, meaning you don't receive a tax deduction for contributions. However, qualified withdrawals, including both contributions and earnings, are tax-free in retirement.

Contribution Limit:

The annual contribution limits for Roth IRAs are the same as traditional IRAs. As of 2024, the contribution limit is $7,000 per year for individuals under 50 years old, and $8,000 for individuals aged 50 and older (including catch-up contributions).

Income eligibility:

Unlike traditional IRAs, which have no income limits for contributions (though they can affect tax deductibility), Roth IRAs do have income limits. In 2024, for single filers, the ability to contribute to a Roth IRA begins to phase out at $146,000 of modified adjusted gross income (MAGI), and contributions are completely phased out at $161,000. For married couples filing jointly, the phase-out begins at $230,000 and contributions are fully phased out at $240,000.

Tax-free growth:
One of the key benefits of a Roth IRA is that investment earnings within the account grow tax-free. This means you won't owe taxes on dividends, interest, or capital gains as long as the funds remain in the Roth IRA.

Tax-free withdrawals in retirement:
Another major advantage of Roth IRAs is that qualified withdrawals in retirement are entirely tax-free. To be considered qualified, withdrawals must meet two basic criteria: the account holder must be at least 59½ years old, and the account must have been open for at least five years. This tax-free withdrawal feature can be incredibly valuable in retirement, as it provides a source of income without the burden of income tax.

Flexibility with withdrawals:
Roth IRAs offer more flexibility with withdrawals compared to traditional IRAs. Contributions (but not earnings) can be withdrawn at any time and for any reason without taxes or penalties, making Roth IRAs a valuable tool for both retirement savings and emergency funds.

Estimating Your Retirement Needs:

One of the first steps in retirement planning is estimating how much money you will need to maintain your desired lifestyle during retirement. Several factors influence your retirement needs, including:

1. Living Expenses:

Estimate your living expenses in retirement, including housing, utilities, food, transportation, healthcare, and discretionary spending. Consider how your expenses may change in retirement, such as lower commuting costs but potentially higher healthcare expenses.

2. Inflation:
Factor in inflation when estimating your retirement needs. Inflation erodes the purchasing power of your money over time, meaning you will need more money in the future to maintain the same standard of living. Use a conservative estimate for inflation, typically around 3% annually.

3. Life Expectancy:
Consider your life expectancy when planning for retirement. While no one can predict exactly how long they will live, estimating your life expectancy based on factors like your health, family history, and lifestyle can help ensure you don't outlive your retirement savings.

4. Social Security and Pension Benefits:
Consider any Social Security benefits or pension income you expect to receive in retirement. These sources of income can supplement your retirement savings and reduce the amount you need to withdraw from your retirement accounts.

Strategies for Catching Up on Retirement Savings:

If you find yourself behind on retirement savings, there are several strategies you can employ to catch up and increase your savings rate. Here are some strategies for catching up on retirement savings:

Increase Contributions:
Maximize your contributions to retirement accounts like 401(k)s and IRAs. Take advantage of catch-up contributions, which allow individuals aged 50 and older to contribute additional funds to

their retirement accounts above the regular contribution limits.

Delay Retirement:
Consider delaying retirement to allow more time for your investments to grow and reduce the number of years you'll need to rely on your retirement savings. Continuing to work also provides an opportunity to boost your retirement savings through additional income and employer contributions.

Reduce Expenses:
Cut back on discretionary expenses and unnecessary spending to free up more money for retirement savings. Look for areas where you can reduce costs, such as dining out less frequently, downsizing your home, or eliminating expensive subscriptions and memberships.

Invest Wisely:
Review your investment strategy and consider reallocating your portfolio to more aggressive investments that offer higher growth potential. However, be mindful of your risk tolerance and investment horizon when making changes to your investment portfolio.

Planning for a Successful Retirement:

Planning for retirement goes beyond saving money—it involves creating a comprehensive retirement plan that addresses various aspects of your financial and lifestyle needs. Here are some key elements of planning for a successful retirement:

Set Clear Goals:
Define your retirement goals and priorities, including when you want to retire, how you envision spending your time in retirement, and any specific financial milestones you want to achieve.

Create a Retirement Budget:
Develop a detailed retirement budget that outlines your expected income sources, expenses, and discretionary spending

in retirement. Factor in inflation, healthcare costs, and other potential expenses to ensure your budget is realistic and sustainable.

Healthcare Planning:
Consider the cost of healthcare in retirement and plan accordingly. Research Medicare coverage options, supplemental insurance plans, and long-term care insurance to protect yourself against unexpected medical expenses.

Estate Planning:
Create or update your estate plan to ensure your assets are distributed according to your wishes and minimize estate taxes. Establish powers of attorney, healthcare directives, and guardianship arrangements to protect yourself and your loved ones in the event of incapacity.

Stay Flexible:
Be prepared to adjust your retirement plan as needed based on changing circumstances, such as market conditions, health issues, or family dynamics. Regularly review and update your retirement plan to stay on track and make necessary adjustments.

Conclusion:

Retirement planning is a complex and multifaceted process that requires careful consideration of various factors, including retirement accounts, estimated retirement needs, strategies for catching up on savings, and planning for a successful retirement. By understanding these key aspects of retirement planning and taking proactive steps to address them, you can set yourself up for a financially secure and fulfilling retirement. Start planning for your retirement today to ensure a brighter tomorrow.

CHAPTER 10 REAL WORLD SCENARIOS

Scenario 1: High School Student

Emily is a 17-year-old high school student who is eager to learn about personal finance and start managing her money responsibly. She understands the importance of financial literacy in achieving her future goals and wants to lay the groundwork for financial success early on.

Solution 1:
Budgeting:
Emily begins by creating a simple budget to track her income and expenses. She lists all sources of income, including allowances, part-time job earnings, or gifts. Emily then identifies her expenses, such as transportation, entertainment, clothing, and savings goals. By tracking her spending, Emily gains insight into her financial habits and learns to prioritize her spending based on her values and goals.

Saving and Goal Setting:
Recognizing the importance of saving for the future, Emily sets specific savings goals for herself. Whether it's saving for college, a car, or a special trip, Emily establishes a plan to set aside a portion of her income regularly. She opens a savings account to keep her money safe and easily accessible while earning interest. Emily sets achievable milestones and celebrates her progress as she works towards her savings goals.

Part-Time Job or Side Hustle:

To increase her income and gain valuable work experience, Emily considers getting a part-time job or starting a side hustle. She explores job opportunities in her community, such as babysitting, tutoring, or working at a local store or restaurant. Emily also considers using her skills and interests to start a small business, such as selling handmade crafts or offering services like dog walking or lawn care.

Understanding Credit and Debt:
As Emily prepares to enter adulthood, she educates herself about credit and debt management. She learns about the importance of maintaining a good credit score and using credit responsibly. Emily understands the risks associated with debt, such as credit card debt or student loans, and strives to avoid excessive borrowing. She explores options for building credit responsibly, such as becoming an authorized user on a parent's credit card or applying for a secured credit card.

Financial Education and Resources:
Emily takes advantage of opportunities to learn about personal finance through her school, community resources, and online resources. She attends workshops, seminars, or classes on topics like budgeting, saving, investing, and managing debt. Emily also seeks guidance from trusted adults, such as parents, teachers, or financial advisors, to gain insights and advice tailored to her unique financial situation and goals.

Practicing Smart Spending Habits:
Emily develops smart spending habits to make the most of her money. She compares prices, looks for deals and discounts, and avoids impulse purchases. Emily also considers the value of purchases relative to her long-term goals, prioritizing spending on items or experiences that align with her values and bring lasting satisfaction. By practicing mindful spending, Emily stretches her dollars further and maximizes her financial resources.

Planning for Higher Education:
As Emily prepares for life after high school, she explores options for financing her college education. She researches scholarships, grants, and financial aid opportunities to help cover tuition, fees, and other expenses. Emily also considers the benefits of attending community college or starting at a four-year university to minimize costs. By planning ahead and being proactive, Emily sets herself up for success in pursuing her educational aspirations without accumulating excessive student loan debt.

By following these steps and adopting a proactive approach to personal finance, Emily sets herself up for financial success as she navigates the transition to adulthood and beyond. She gains valuable skills and knowledge that will serve her well in managing her money responsibly and achieving her long-term goals.

Scenario 2: College Graduate

Maya is a 25-year-old recent college graduate who has just started her first full-time job. She's excited about her newfound financial independence but also feels overwhelmed by the responsibility of managing her finances. Maya wants to make smart financial decisions to set herself up for long-term success but isn't sure where to start.

Solution 2:
Budgeting:
Maya begins by creating a budget to track her income and expenses. She lists all sources of income, including her salary and any additional income from freelance work or side gigs. Then, she identifies her fixed expenses (rent, utilities, transportation, groceries) and discretionary expenses (entertainment, dining out, shopping). By budgeting carefully, Maya ensures that she's living within her means and has enough money left over for savings and other financial goals.

Building an Emergency Fund:
Understanding the importance of having a financial safety net, Maya decides to prioritize building an emergency fund. She aims to save at least three to six months' worth of living expenses in a high-yield savings account. Maya contributes a portion of each paycheck to her emergency fund until she reaches her goal, providing peace of mind in case of unexpected expenses like car repairs or medical bills.

Paying Off Student Loans:
Like many recent graduates, Maya has student loan debt from her college education. She reviews her loan terms, including interest rates and repayment options, and creates a plan to pay off her loans efficiently. Maya considers strategies such as making extra payments toward the principal, refinancing at a lower interest rate if possible, or exploring loan forgiveness programs based on her career field.

Saving for Retirement:
Even though retirement may seem far off, Maya understands the importance of starting to save early. She enrolls in her employer's retirement plan, such as a 401(k) or 403(b), and contributes enough to take full advantage of any employer matching contributions. Maya also educates herself about investment options within her retirement account and chooses a diversified portfolio aligned with her risk tolerance and long-term goals.

Investing for the Future:
In addition to saving for retirement, Maya wants to invest for other financial goals, such as buying a home or traveling. She opens a brokerage account and begins investing in low-cost index funds or exchange-traded funds (ETFs) to build wealth over time. Maya understands the power of compound interest and commits to regular contributions to her investment portfolio, leveraging the potential for long-term growth.

Continuing Financial Education:

Recognizing that personal finance is an ongoing journey, Maya makes a commitment to continue educating herself about financial topics. She reads books, listens to podcasts, and follows reputable financial websites to stay informed about budgeting, investing, taxes, and other aspects of personal finance. Maya also seeks guidance from financial professionals when needed to make informed decisions about her financial future.

By implementing these strategies, Maya takes control of her finances and lays the foundation for a secure and prosperous future as a young adult.

Scenario 3: Starting a Family

Sarah and John are both 28 years old and recently got married. They're excited about starting a family but recognize the need to manage their finances wisely to provide for their future children and achieve their long-term goals. They want to ensure financial stability and security as they navigate this new chapter of their lives.

Solution 3:
Combining Finances:
Sarah and John begin by discussing their financial goals and merging their finances. They open a joint checking account for shared expenses like rent/mortgage, utilities, groceries, and childcare expenses. They also maintain separate individual accounts for personal spending and savings.

Creating a Family Budget:
Together, Sarah and John create a comprehensive family budget to track their combined income and expenses. They list all sources of income, including salaries, bonuses, and any additional income from side hustles or investments. They then identify fixed expenses (e.g., housing, utilities, insurance premiums) and variable expenses (e.g., groceries, entertainment, transportation). Sarah and John allocate funds for savings, debt repayment, and

future goals, ensuring they're living within their means and saving for their growing family's needs.

Building an Emergency Fund:
Recognizing the importance of financial stability, Sarah and John prioritize building an emergency fund to cover unexpected expenses. They aim to save at least six months' worth of living expenses in a joint high-yield savings account. They contribute a portion of each paycheck to their emergency fund until they reach their goal, providing a financial safety net for their family in case of job loss, medical emergencies, or other unforeseen circumstances.

Planning for Childbirth and Parental Leave:
With plans to start a family, Sarah and John research the costs associated with childbirth, including prenatal care, delivery, and postnatal expenses. They review their health insurance coverage to understand their benefits and out-of-pocket costs. Sarah and John also discuss parental leave policies with their employers and develop a plan to manage their finances during any unpaid leave periods, considering options like using accrued vacation time, paid family leave benefits, or temporary adjustments to their budget.
Some employers do not offer any paid leave benefits. Make sure to review the short-term disability policy. If your employer doesn't automatically enroll you in the policy, make sure to opt in the year you plan on having a child to get 60% of your paycheck for 6 weeks following childbirth.

Saving for Future Expenses:
In anticipation of the additional expenses that come with raising a child, Sarah and John start saving for future needs like childcare, education, and healthcare. They open a separate savings account specifically earmarked for their child's expenses and contribute regularly to build up these funds over time. They also explore tax-advantaged savings vehicles like 529 college savings plans to save for their child's education expenses.

Reviewing Insurance Coverage:
As they start a family, Sarah and John review their insurance coverage to ensure adequate protection for their loved ones. They update their health insurance policies to include coverage for dependents and consider additional insurance options like life insurance and disability insurance to provide financial security in case of illness, injury, or death.

Estate Planning:
Sarah and John understand the importance of estate planning, especially now that they're starting a family. They consult with an estate planning attorney to draft essential documents like wills, trusts, and powers of attorney. They designate guardians for their child in case of incapacitation or death and outline their wishes for the distribution of assets and the care of their family members.

Adjusting Long-Term Financial Goals:
With the addition of a new family member, Sarah, and John revisit their long-term financial goals and adjust their plans accordingly. They may need to reprioritize goals like homeownership, retirement savings, and career advancement to accommodate the needs of their growing family. Sarah and John discuss their aspirations together and develop a roadmap for achieving their shared financial objectives while providing for their family's well-being.

By taking proactive steps to manage their finances, Sarah and John set a solid foundation for their family's financial future, ensuring stability, security, and prosperity as they embark on this exciting journey of starting a family together.

Scenario 4: Middle Aged

Paul is a 45-year-old married man with two children, aged 14 and 16. He and his wife are navigating the challenges of managing their finances while juggling their children's education, extracurricular activities, and household expenses. Paul wants to ensure that he's adequately preparing for his family's future while also enjoying their present life together.

Solution 4:
College Savings:
With college tuition costs continuing to rise, Paul and his wife prioritize saving for their children's education. They contribute regularly to 529 college savings plans for each child, taking advantage of tax benefits and investment growth potential. Paul research various investment options within the 529 plans to align with their risk tolerance and timeline for college expenses.

Retirement Planning:
As Paul approaches his fifties, retirement planning becomes a top priority. He maximizes contributions to his employer-sponsored retirement accounts, such as a 401(k) or 403(b), and considers additional retirement savings vehicles like IRAs. Paul evaluates his retirement savings progress against his retirement goals, adjusting his contributions and investment allocations as needed to stay on track for a comfortable retirement.

Life Insurance and Estate Planning:
Recognizing the importance of protecting his family's financial future, Paul reviews his life insurance coverage to ensure it's sufficient to provide for his family in case of his untimely death. He also revisits his estate plan, updating his will, trust documents, and beneficiary designations to reflect his current wishes and provide for his children's inheritance and guardianship.

Health and Disability Insurance:
Paul ensures that his family has comprehensive health insurance coverage to protect against medical expenses and unexpected healthcare costs. He reviews their health insurance policy's coverage details and considers supplemental coverage options like dental and vision insurance. Paul also explores disability insurance to replace his income in case of injury or illness that prevents him from working.

Financial Education for Children:
Paul and his wife prioritize teaching their children about money management and financial responsibility. They involve their children in discussions about family finances, budgeting, saving, and investing. Paul encourages his children to open their own savings accounts and learn the value of saving for short-term goals like buying a car or long-term goals like saving for college or retirement.

Career Development and Income Growth:
Paul evaluates his career trajectory and considers opportunities for professional development and advancement that could increase his earning potential and job security. He invests in continuing education, skills training, or networking opportunities to stay competitive in his field and position himself for future career growth. Paul also explores potential side hustles or entrepreneurial ventures to supplement his income and build additional financial security for his family.

Balancing Present Enjoyment with Future Planning:
While planning is essential, Paul and his family also prioritize enjoying their present life together. They allocate funds for family vacations, experiences, and quality time together, balancing their financial goals with opportunities to create lasting memories and strengthen family bonds. Paul finds fulfillment in striking a balance between providing for his family's future and cherishing the moments they share today.

By implementing these strategies, Paul manages the complexities of mid-life financial planning while prioritizing his family's needs and aspirations, setting the stage for a secure and fulfilling future for himself and his loved ones.

Scenario 5: Retirement

Mary is a 62-year-old professional who has spent decades working in her career and is now considering retirement. As she approaches retirement age, Mary wants to ensure that she has enough savings and financial resources to support her desired lifestyle during retirement. She's also mindful of healthcare costs, social security benefits, and estate planning considerations as she prepares to transition into retirement.

Solution:
Retirement Savings Assessment:
Mary begins by assessing her retirement savings and investment accounts to determine if she has enough saved to retire comfortably. She evaluates her employer-sponsored retirement accounts, such as a 401(k) or 403(b), as well as any individual retirement accounts (IRAs) or other investment accounts. Mary reviews her retirement savings goals, projected expenses, and expected retirement age to gauge her readiness for retirement.

Social Security Planning:
Mary explores her options for claiming Social Security benefits and considers the optimal timing for starting to receive benefits. She reviews her Social Security statement to estimate her future benefits based on her earnings history and retirement age. Mary evaluates factors like life expectancy, spousal benefits, and the impact of delaying or accelerating her Social Security claiming decision on her overall retirement income.

Healthcare and Long-Term Care Planning:
Recognizing the potential impact of healthcare costs on her retirement budget, Mary investigates healthcare options available to retirees, such as Medicare, supplemental insurance plans (Medigap), and Medicare Advantage plans. She estimates her out-of-pocket healthcare expenses, including premiums, deductibles, copayments, and prescription drug costs, and factors these into her retirement budget. Mary also considers long-term care insurance to protect against the high costs of nursing home or home healthcare services in later years.

Retirement Income Sources:

Mary examines her sources of retirement income beyond savings and Social Security benefits. She considers potential income streams such as pension benefits from her employer, rental income from investment properties, dividends from stocks or bonds, or part-time employment during retirement. Mary evaluates the reliability and sustainability of each income source and incorporates them into her retirement income plan.

Estate Planning and Legacy Considerations:
As Mary approaches retirement, she revisits her estate plan to ensure that her wishes are documented, and her assets are distributed according to her preferences. She updates her will, establishes trusts, designates beneficiaries for retirement accounts and insurance policies, and considers strategies to minimize estate taxes and probate costs. Mary also communicates her estate plan with her family members and seeks guidance from legal and financial professionals to ensure that her legacy goals are met.

Lifestyle and Retirement Goals:
Mary reflects on her retirement lifestyle goals and considers how she envisions spending her time in retirement. She evaluates factors like travel plans, hobbies, volunteer work, and spending on leisure activities and entertainment. Mary balances her retirement aspirations with financial realities, adjusting her budget and savings strategies as needed to align with her retirement goals and priorities.

Financial Advisory and Retirement Planning Services:
Recognizing the complexity of retirement planning, Mary seeks guidance from financial advisors or retirement planning professionals to help her navigate key decisions and optimize her retirement strategy. She collaborates with advisors to develop a comprehensive retirement plan tailored to her unique financial situation, goals, and risk tolerance. Mary regularly reviews and adjusts her retirement plan as she approaches retirement and throughout her retirement years to adapt to changing

circumstances and market conditions.

By following these steps and proactively planning for retirement, Mary sets herself up for a secure and fulfilling retirement experience, enabling her to enjoy the fruits of her labor and achieve her desired lifestyle goals in her golden years.

Managing personal finance is a lifelong journey that evolves through various stages of life, each presenting unique challenges, opportunities, and priorities. From the early years of building financial literacy and laying the groundwork for future success to the later stages of retirement planning and legacy considerations, individuals must navigate different financial milestones and transitions with foresight, discipline, and adaptability.

CHAPTER 11: ACHIEVING FINANCIAL FREEDOM

Financial freedom is a goal many aspire to achieve—a state where one has enough wealth and resources to live comfortably, pursue passions, and enjoy life without being constrained by financial concerns. While the path to financial freedom may seem daunting, it is attainable with careful planning, disciplined execution, and a mindset geared towards abundance. In this chapter, we'll explore the various aspects of achieving financial freedom, including assessing your progress, strategies for accelerating your journey, overcoming common obstacles, and embracing a wealth mindset.

Assessing Your Progress Toward Financial Independence:

Assessing your progress toward financial independence is a crucial step in your journey towards financial freedom. It involves taking stock of your current financial situation, understanding your goals, and evaluating whether you are on track to achieve them. Here are some key components of assessing your progress:

Net Worth Calculation:

Your net worth is a snapshot of your financial health and represents the difference between your assets and liabilities. Assets include savings, investments, property, and other valuable possessions, while liabilities encompass debts and financial obligations. Calculating your net worth periodically allows you to track your progress over time and identify areas for improvement.

Income and Expenses Analysis:

Understanding your cash flow is essential for assessing your financial progress. Analyze your income sources, including wages, investments, and other sources of revenue, as well as your expenses, such as housing, transportation, food, and discretionary spending. Identifying areas where you can increase income or reduce expenses can help boost your savings rate and accelerate your journey to financial freedom.

Debt Management:
Debt can be a significant obstacle on the path to financial freedom, so it's essential to assess your debt levels and develop a plan to pay off high-interest debt. Prioritize debt repayment based on interest rates and focus on reducing or eliminating debts that are hindering your financial progress. Consider strategies like the debt snowball or debt avalanche method to accelerate debt repayment and free up cash flow for saving and investing.

Emergency Fund:
Building an emergency fund is a critical aspect of financial independence, providing a financial safety net to cover unexpected expenses or emergencies. Evaluate the adequacy of your emergency fund and aim to save at least three to six months' worth of living expenses in a liquid, easily accessible account. Having a robust emergency fund ensures you can weather financial storms without derailing your long-term goals.

Strategies for Accelerating Your Journey to Financial Freedom:

While achieving financial freedom requires patience and discipline, there are strategies you can employ to accelerate your progress and reach your goals sooner. Here are some effective strategies for accelerating your journey to financial freedom:

Increase Income:
Boosting your income is one of the most effective ways to accelerate your journey to financial freedom. Look for opportunities to increase your earning potential through career

advancement, side hustles, freelancing, or entrepreneurship. Consider acquiring new skills, pursuing advanced education or certifications, or exploring higher-paying job opportunities to increase your income streams.

Maximize Savings:
Saving aggressively is essential for building wealth and achieving financial freedom. Maximize your savings rate by automating your savings, setting specific savings goals, and prioritizing long-term financial objectives. Cut unnecessary expenses, live below your means, and avoid lifestyle inflation to increase your savings rate and accelerate your journey to financial independence.

Invest Wisely:
Investing wisely is key to building wealth and achieving financial freedom. Develop a diversified investment portfolio aligned with your risk tolerance, time horizon, and financial goals. Consider investing in low-cost index funds, exchange-traded funds (ETFs), mutual funds, individual stocks, bonds, real estate, and other asset classes to maximize returns and minimize risk. Regularly review and rebalance your investment portfolio to ensure it remains aligned with your objectives and risk tolerance.

Real Estate Investments:
Real estate can be a powerful wealth-building tool and an effective strategy for accelerating your journey to financial freedom. Explore real estate investments, such as rental properties, house hacking, real estate investment trusts (REITs), crowdfunding platforms, and fix-and-flip opportunities. Real estate investments offer various benefits, including passive income, tax advantages, diversification, and potential appreciation, making them an attractive option for building wealth over time.

Overcoming Common Obstacles:

Achieving financial freedom is not without its challenges, and overcoming common obstacles is essential for staying on track and reaching your goals. Here are some common obstacles you may encounter on your journey to financial freedom and strategies for overcoming them:

Debt:
Debt can be a significant barrier to financial freedom, so it's essential to prioritize debt repayment and eliminate high-interest debt as quickly as possible. Develop a debt repayment plan, focus on paying off debts with the highest interest rates first, and consider debt consolidation or refinancing to lower interest costs and accelerate debt payoff.

Lack of Financial Literacy:
Financial literacy is critical for making informed decisions about money and achieving financial independence. Educate yourself about personal finance topics, including budgeting, saving, investing, retirement planning, and debt management. Take advantage of resources such as books, online courses, podcasts, workshops, and financial advisors to enhance your financial knowledge and skills.

Emotional Spending:
Emotional spending can derail your progress toward financial freedom by leading to impulse purchases, overspending, and lifestyle inflation. Practice mindful spending, differentiate between needs and wants, and avoid making impulsive financial decisions. Develop healthy spending habits, set spending limits, and create a budget that aligns with your financial goals and values.

Fear and Uncertainty:
Fear and uncertainty can paralyze you and prevent you from acting toward achieving your financial goals. Cultivate a growth mindset, focus on what you can control, and embrace challenges as opportunities for growth and learning. Seek support from friends, family, mentors, or a financial advisor to help you navigate challenges and overcome obstacles on your journey to financial freedom.

Embracing a Wealth Mindset:

Embracing a wealth mindset is essential for achieving financial freedom and creating abundance in your life. A wealth mindset involves cultivating positive beliefs, attitudes, and behaviors related to money and success. Here are some principles of a wealth mindset:

Abundance Mentality:
Adopt an abundance mindset and believe that there is more than enough wealth and opportunity to go around. Focus on abundance rather than scarcity and cultivate gratitude for what you have. Trust that you have the resources, skills, and abilities to achieve your financial goals and create the life you desire.

Financial Goals:
Set clear financial goals and visualize your desired outcomes to align your actions with your aspirations. Break down big goals into smaller, manageable steps and celebrate your progress along the way. Set specific, measurable, achievable, relevant, and time-bound (SMART) goals to stay focused and motivated on your journey to financial freedom.

Positive Self-Talk:
Monitor your thoughts and beliefs about money and challenge any negative or limiting beliefs that hold you back. Practice positive self-talk and affirmations to reprogram your subconscious mind for success and abundance. Replace negative thoughts with empowering beliefs and affirmations that support your financial goals and aspirations.

Continuous Learning:
Commit to lifelong learning and personal growth to expand your knowledge, skills, and abilities. Invest in yourself through education, self-improvement, and skill development to increase your earning potential and achieve greater success. Stay curious, open-minded, and adaptable, and embrace challenges as opportunities for growth and learning.

Conclusion:

Achieving financial freedom is a journey that requires dedication, discipline, and a wealth mindset. By assessing your progress, employing strategies to accelerate your journey, overcoming common obstacles, and embracing a mindset geared towards abundance, you can create the financial freedom and abundance you desire. Start acting today to build the life of your dreams and live with purpose, passion, and prosperity. Remember that financial freedom is not just about achieving wealth—it's about creating a life of freedom, fulfillment, and joy.

ABOUT THE AUTHOR

David Klipsch

David Klipsch became interested in personal finance when he graduated from college and was stuck under a pile of debt. After paying off $70,000 in student loan debt in just two years, he continued learning about personal finance and investing. Through the knowledge he obtained, his friends asked him to give a presentation on personal finance and investing to help them improve their financial situations. This motivated David to write this book to educate and inspire more people to take control of their finances.

www.ingramcontent.com/pod-product-compliance
Lightning Source LLC
Chambersburg PA
CBHW070342230526
45471CB00006B/2420